Curveballs

Curveballs

By
Catherine A. Mardon

Edited by
Austin A. Mardon

Golden Meteorite Press

A Golden Meteorite Press Book.

© 2008 copyright by Catherine Mardon, Canada. All rights reserved. No part of this work may be reproduced in any form or by any means, electronic or mechanical, including photocopying, recording, taping, or any retrieval system, without the written permission of Golden Meteorite Press at ccmardon@yahoo.ca. Printed in Canada. Published by Golden Meteorite Press.

ISBN 978-1-897472-02-3

Library and Archives Canada Cataloguing in Publication:

Mardon, Catherine A., 1962-
    Curveballs / Catherine A. Mardon ; Austin A. Mardon, editor.

ISBN 978-1-897472-03-3

    I. Mardon, Austin A. (Austin Albert) II. Title.

PS3613.A738C87 2008   813'.6   C2008-901886-9

Dedicated to

My father whom I still miss everyday, and to Paul and Ralph who were always there when I needed them just as they promised.

Acknowledgements:

I want to thank my beloved husband for pushing me when I need it, and catching me when I fall. A big hug and thanks to Carol, Joelle, and John for being willing to read this in its raw form. Extreme thanks to Anne who spent hours on the phone and computer making sure my head was actually screwed on straight. Appreciations to Sr. Diane Koorie and the Archdiocese of Oklahoma City for allowing me to finish my pastoral ministry degree by distance education, extreme distance. Heartfelt thanks to the men and women of St. Al's for being so welcoming to someone with a really strange accent. Thanks to Janet for the loan of her couch. To my Baby Brother, thanks for allowing the world's most bratty little sister to have some one to look up to and be so very proud of. Finally to Canadian Immigration, thanks for finally agreeing that I was not a terrorist.

Based on a true story.

The names and places have been changed to protect the innocent from the guilty. All material is based on eyewitness accounts, medical reports, and the slowly reconstructed damaged memory of the author.

Prologue

My father was a baseball fan. He had grown up in New York City during the Babe Ruth era. What else could he have been? He once told me that in life, you either learn to throw the curveball, or you have to learn to hit one, or you can't play the game. If it seemed strange that he was teaching his youngest child, and only daughter to throw a curveball at the age of 10, he never seemed to notice. He was 57 years old at the time, recovering from a heart attack. He was strong enough to play in the back yard with me, but not allowed to go back to work yet.

I learned well the lessons of my childhood. I still use them on a daily basis. This is a story about the person I was, the person I couldn't help becoming, and the person I strive to be now. It's about idealism, ambition, retribution and salvation. The Lord has thrown a lot of curveballs at me over the years. Some I've seen coming. Some have knocked me off the plate. One actually beaned me. Every now and then, God throws me a meatball, usually when I need it the most.

Curveballs

Curveballs

Chapter 1: Making a Mold

My parents were old enough to be my grandparents. I was actually closer in age to my nieces and nephews than I was to most of my older brothers. I was even younger than the children of some of my cousins. I told an old friend recently, who also had much older parents growing up, that we had the advantage of learning skills from our parents that our peers with much younger parents missed out on. The trade off is that we grew up knowing that our parents wouldn't be around for us as long. I figured up once that my mother had 34 more birthdays and Father's days with her father than I had with mine, but I'd like to think that the years I had, I grabbed a lifetime's worth of his wisdom and strength.

My dad had been a war hero. Not the kind of hero that everyone knows about because his medals are displayed prominently, or because he gives interviews, but the kind of hero who can't talk about what he did, and hides his medals at the back of his sock drawer. That's where I found them when I was a child. The colors on all the medals looked like Christmas ribbons. I wondered what they were for. Never being afraid of asking questions as a child, most of the time too many questions, I asked him what they meant. He just said, "A man shouldn't be given an award just for being left alive." Then he put the box back in his drawer where I had found it. From time to time I would take them out and look at them and wonder. They had a musty smell like a basement. I never guessed at their significance until years later, even though the evidence was all around me.

How many fathers teach their daughters to box at the age of 6? To me it just meant spending time with him. He worked very hard at a job that kept him outside most of the time, and in Oklahoma that meant freezing in winter and boiling in summer. By the time I came along, he was not just older, he was very tired. He once told me it wasn't the years, it was the miles. His father had died when he was 6 months old. His mother followed 3 years later when the Spanish Flu decimated the rest of his family. His brother died in the street in front of his eyes when he was 5 years old. He was raised by his

Curveballs

poor, widowed, grandmother during the depression. Then the war came. After my father died, I remember going through his papers. I found a bunch of disjointed Army paperwork. On one sheet it had listed some testing the Army had done on him. His IQ at the time was 156. He had wanted to go to flight school, but his eyesight wasn't good enough. He could have gone to Officer's Candidate School, except he had dropped out of high school when his grandmother had become ill to support the family. So the Army sent him where they sent smart people who couldn't fly or be officers, to radio school. He learned Morse code and was assigned to a bomber squadron in a Lend/Lease unit in the South Atlantic. A year before Pearl Harbor, he was already in the war chasing U-boats. After the US entered the war, his record basically disappears. We were told he had been in the OSS, and that we shouldn't ask anymore questions. I woke many nights to the sounds of my father screaming in his sleep. Deep down, I guess I really didn't want to know.

Chapter 2: The Matriarch

Where my father was a mystery, my mother was an open book. She had come from a prominent family of merchants. Her ancestors had been at Jamestown. She was descended from Kings and Queens, and founders of the country. The fact that she had married a poor veteran from an equally poor family seemed to haunt her. She was supposed to have married someone much different. She lived her entire life like someone that was supposed to have had more. That resulted in her pushing me to have the life that she was meant to have and had been cheated out of. I'm not sure what that life was supposed to have been exactly, but I had to not only "do" everything that came along, I had to be the best at it.

While my father was teaching me to box, my mother was signing me up for tap dance lessons. I had been in my first beauty pageant when I was just 3 years old. The second place finish didn't dissuade her in any way. She had waited two decades to finally have a girl, and was determined that I become a proper Southern Belle. She had been a debutant, and couldn't understand why I wanted a different path. As soon as I was old enough to dress myself, the pink lace went out the window in favor of jeans and t-shirts. Years later when my mother lamented about not getting to make me frilly dresses anymore, I asked her what she expected from me being raised around all those boys. Not only did I have no sisters, there were not even any girls on my block for me to play with. If I wanted to be able to play with the neighborhood kids, I had to play cops and robbers, not dolls.

This latent tomboyism didn't keep my mother from pressing me in every other aspect of my life. In first grade, it was Blue Birds. I couldn't just have fun with my school friends; I had to be the best Blue Bird. I had to sell the most candy, and earn the most badges. I was enrolled in summer musicals put on by the parks and recreation department. I had a big voice and a large stage presence. When I was old enough for band and athletics, I wasn't allowed to choose which one I would prefer, I was expected to do both. I couldn't just make the basketball team; I had to be first string. I couldn't just enjoy being in the band, I had to become first chair. As it went with many things in my life, I wasn't even allowed to choose my instrument. I played trombone, because one of my older brothers had played, and that was just one of many masculine hand-me-downs I would endure.

I was blessed/cursed with my father's IQ. I was such a curious child, that it took almost constant supervision to keep me from harm. When I was barely 8, I decided to take my parent's alarm clock apart. I did it several more times, each time getting more pieces off before putting it back together. Finally, inevitably, I ended up with an extra piece left over. My mother thought that her clock had just quit working. I'm not sure how my father eventually found out that I had been doing surgery on items around the house, but that summer he obtained from a neighbor who worked for the phone company a large box of broken phones. He used them for spare parts, and had more than enough, so I was happily knee deep in phone parts for months. I ended up making several working models from the carcasses and parts.

My grandmother was upset when my grandfather retired, so she decided to get a job to get out of the house. She went to work at high scale women's department store in the hosiery department. She got access to boxes of broken costume jewelry. That was my next project, learning to fix broken jewelry. The nuns at school had shown me how to make rosaries, and I loved taking broken jewelry from my devout Baptist grandmother and turning them into rosaries. I literally tinkered with anything I could get my hands on. I still do that.

My parents were willing to let me try things that other parents would have been scared to. I don't know if it was because they knew I was smart enough to get myself out of most tight spots, or if it was because they were too tired to fight me. I actually started doing their taxes when I was just 12 years old. My parents were getting audited because their tax person had messed something up. They made the mistake of leaving the tax forms out on the table to be redone. When they got back home, I had redone them correctly. I got to do their taxes every year after that.

I did so many dangerous things just to push my limits. I drove way too fast at times, went camping in remote areas by myself as soon as I got my driver's license, and pulled all sorts of stunts. I started working at a movie theatre at 14, and volunteered to be the person who confronted people smoking or drinking alcohol in the building. I tried out for a professional women's football team, and would have gotten a chance to play had they not found out I was underage. One of my most endearing qualities is that I was always looking for a fight. I was so competitive at everything. My mother's pushing me to be the best at everything I tried had made its impression permanently on my soul.

I seemed to be especially fearless when it came to things that would give other normal children pause. I could usually think my way out of most situations, but there was one that I almost didn't walk away from. I had a great sled growing up. Oklahoma doesn't have the longest or hardest winters, but we usually got at least one really good snow storm every year. When it came, we always felt like we needed to take advantage while the snow was flying. The winter I turned 10 years old I was engrossed in the winter Olympics in Japan. I especially liked the luge. I decided to take my sled to what we called the creek. It was actually a large capacity concrete storm water drainage canal. It was over 20 feet deep and 20 feet across at the bottom.

The sides were sloped pretty steeply, but I had never had any problem climbing up or down. I knew in winter the water at the bottom would be frozen. Except for after large storms, it was rarely more than 6 inches deep. Its twists and turns reminded me of the luge track, and I just had to give it a try. I took a neighborhood friend with me. We were sledding at enormous speeds for almost two hours before we started to feel really cold. Then we came to the realization that the sides which had been so easy to go down, were much harder to go back up. Normally in summer the roughness of the concrete gave us more than enough friction to climb back out. With the sides covered in ice, it was impossible. I was strong enough to lift my friend up on my shoulders high

Curveballs

enough that she could grab the branches of a seedling to pull herself out, but I was stuck without help from someone older, so I asked her to go get my mom. I waited quite a long time before realizing that the half block trip to my house and back should have already happened. As the winter sun began to deepen, I realized that I was on my own. I started walking along the canal looking for a better way out. We had always just played in our own area. Had I walked just two blocks North, I would have found that the section of the canal that had been concreted to prevent erosion just started there. I could have easily climbed up the dirt and grass covered sides. I instead stated walking south. South was a direction I knew. It was the direction of my Godmother's house. The creek actually came up to the fence in her back yard.

    I walked the 6 blocks south, shivering from the cold, and long since unable to feel my feet. When I got to her back yard, I began to use all the energy I had left to scream for help. Someone next door heard me, and rang my Godmother's bell. They were able to get me out with the help of a rope. I warmed up in her kitchen with some Mexican hot chocolate and some warm towels on my feet. My feet were mostly bright red, but the tips of my toes were white like I had spent too much time in the bath tub. When I started to be able to feel them again, they hurt like a thousand bee stings. I had been wearing an old ski mask that exposed my lips and eyes. They were also bright red with spots of white. Within days, the skin would peel from my lips leaving large scabs forever immortalized in my school pictures that year.

    When she drove me home finally, I found my sled in our front yard right where my friend had left it. I discovered later that she had been too afraid of my mother to knock on the door for help. My mother had not even noticed that I had been gone. Some people talk about being abused or neglected. I was mostly ignored. By the time I came along, my parents weren't just older, they were tired. I have often wondered what would have happened if I had succumbed to the exposure and hypothermia. I guess they would have eventually noticed that I was gone after my father had come home from work.

Chapter 3: My Guadalupe

My Godmother was also a major influence in my life. She had been an immigrant from Mexico. Her parents crossed the border when she was just 6 months old during the 1920's because of the civil unrest in their home country. She lived her entire life as an alien in a land that was not her home, yet she made it so. She raised 5 children, all who received advanced college degrees. She was the American melting pot. She treated me as just another one of her children. I knew when things were difficult at home that I could find a place at her kitchen table.

She seemed to follow me wherever I went. She worked in the school cafeteria at my parochial school, and coincidently moved to work in the cafeteria at my high school the year that I moved up. She seemed to know what my report cards said before I did. I remember many mornings, when trying to make that difficult transition to high school, going to the cafeteria before school started to watch her prepare the dough for the daily baking. I could talk to her about things that I knew I couldn't with my mother. I hadn't wanted to go to the public high school, but our family just couldn't afford the tuition at the Catholic high school where most of my friends had gone. I guess we had done good to afford the grade school tuition.

While preparing for my confirmation, I began to feel called to the religious life. I tried talking to my mother about entering a religious order, but that wasn't part of her plan for me. At first she laughed, then she became angry, then she refused to speak to me for weeks. I could talk to my Godmother about it though. She had a word with my parochial school principal who was a Carmelite nun. Most of the rest of the sisters at the school were members of the Sisters of Charity. It was unusual to have more than one order in the same school. Between them, they found a Catholic prep-school run by the Benedictines that was willing to give me a full scholarship for high school. The hitch was that it was in Kansas. That was many hours away, and also not in my mother's plans for me.

I knew there was no way that they could talk her into letting me go. Everyone tried, even our pastor, but she refused to discuss it with them. My father, usually so strong, always yielded to my mother's wishes when it came to me. I don't know if it was to forestall a fight, or just because he though as a girl, my mom would know what was best for me. The last attempt was by my Godmother. They actually got into a screaming fight. I have heard my mother raise her voice many times, but not my Godmother. She even started screaming in Spanish, which probably wasn't too helpful since my mother didn't speak Spanish. In the end, she gave up as well, and I resigned myself to attending the public high school.

I didn't give up on my idea of entering a religious order; I just confined my discussions about it to my father and my Godmother. My dad's take on it was that he didn't care what I wanted to be. He said that he didn't care if I wanted to be a garbage man as long as I was happy, and tried to be the best garbage man I could be. My Godmother took it upon herself to educate me the best she could on the things that I would be missing out on by not attending a Catholic high school. Our church had CCD classes on Saturday for kids who weren't in the Catholic school, but my mother didn't want me taking any further religious classes. I would go to school early, and we would discuss theology while she made bread dough. She took being my Godmother, sponsor, very seriously. We talked about what kind of order I wanted to enter, or what kind of ministry I wanted to be involved with. I never had a preference of what kind of order I wanted to enter, but I knew I wanted to do missionary work.

She had taken me to Mexico over breaks or vacations to visit her relatives. I knew what third world countries looked like, and understood the hardships the people living there endured. I hadn't been sheltered from that like most of my suburban neighborhood friends. I wanted to plant trees and build schools. I wanted to take care of the sick or orphaned. She told me that most missionary sisters were nurses. So she wanted me to take as many math and science classes as I could, and learn a foreign language. At that time we

Curveballs

weren't required to take languages to graduate. I wanted to take Spanish, but she encouraged me to take French. She said I could already speak enough Spanish, and that many missions were in French speaking regions. So I took French and Biology and Chemistry. I did well.

My mother was quite excited by my freshmen grades. In parochial school we hadn't received letter grades and grade point averages. She liked being able to wave my grades in the faces of her family members who had always looked down their noses at us for going to Catholic schools. My grades encouraged my mother that I could be the first one in her family to attend college since my great uncle who was a doctor. That just turned up the pressure on me. The idea of maybe going to nursing school went out the window. She wanted me to be a doctor.

Chapter 4: My first real injury

I had never expected high school to be easy. One of the hardest days happened in just the first semester. My high school was to play the Catholic high school that all my friends had gone to. Although I was just a freshman, I was going to be a starting guard. I had never competed against friends before. We had won city and state championships together, and now I was wondering if I would be able to play the game without accidentally throwing one of them the ball out of old habit. As it turned out, none of my old friends even played. Some had given up basketball, some had not made the team as freshmen, and some sat on the bench. We won, but in a real way, that day made me realize that I had entered a whole new place, physically and mentally.

I struggled to stay healthy enough to stay on the various teams. I had torn ligaments in my right ankle playing basketball when I was 13. I re-injured it again once playing basketball, softball and tennis. I hurt it once playing basketball in the driveway, and laid there for over an hour before my brother Jimmy came home and carried me inside. He and I had given each other such grief growing up, but I can still feel how tenderly he cradled me in his arms that night as he carried me inside.

The doctor wanted to reconstruct it. It was a new surgery where he would transplant a tendon from my leg into my ankle to replace the damaged ligaments. Finally the summer I turned 16, I couldn't put the surgery off any longer. My mom moved into my hospital room with her crocheting. She may not have expressed her feelings easily, but she always showed us she cared when we needed it the most. I was given the anointing of the sick the night before the surgery. It scared me at first, but the hospital's chaplain was a wonderful priest that I would see many times again, unfortunately. He explained that the anointing wasn't just for people near death, but also to protect me in case something happened while I was under anesthetic, to strengthen me for my recovery, and to help ease any fear I might be feeling.

Curveballs

I don't really think I was scared before the surgery. They were very good at dealing with kids at St. Anthony's. When I woke up after the surgery, that's when I became afraid. I was in a pain that I can only describe as white, and I was confronted with an enormous cast that was soaked through with blood. It wasn't a walking cast either. I would not be allowed to put any weight on it for months. The next day, they did cut a hole in the cast to allow the dressing to be changed, kind of like an L shaped porthole. When the stitches were removed in a couple of weeks, they just plastered the porthole closed. This was summertime in Oklahoma, and that cast really began to smell after a few weeks.

I learned how to drive my car left footed. I adjusted to being on crutches. I developed calluses in my under arms. Starting my sophomore year in high school on crutches was a challenge, especially since I had to navigate 2 flights of stairs for my math and English classes. I assumed that as soon as the cast finally came off, that I could just go back to all my activities like nothing had changed. I kept score for the softball team that fall, and helped with the equipment. The trainer and I were counting the days until the cast came off. When the doctor finally cut it off, it was moldy and green inside. I'm lucky I didn't get some kind of flesh eating disease. I didn't keep the cast to bronze. I never wanted to see it again.

With the cast off, I got to see my leg for the first time in months. It was white, almost gooey looking, and the hair was almost long enough to braid, but I couldn't take my eyes off the horrific looking red scar. It was a foot long down my leg and across my ankle. I expected to just put my shoe on, which I had of course brought with me, and hop out the door to basketball practice. It didn't work that way. I couldn't stand on it at all. I couldn't bend it even. My world deflated.

I eventually spent another several months on crutches, and even more months walking with a cane. The rehab was slow, painful, and unending. It had cost me the job at the movie theater, and two sports seasons already. I stopped using the cane only after someone at school made fun of me needing a Seeing Eye dog too. I just limped instead. It was well over a year before I felt normal again. I vividly remember the first time I twisted that ankle after the reconstruction. I stepped in a gopher hole, and it buckled. I fell to the ground waiting for the pain to hit, and then it didn't. My ankle was fine. I just sat there on the ground laughing. I went to see the coach the next day. Except for the scar the only way I can tell that anything was ever done to it, is when I am laying on my stomach. That foot won't lie as completely flat as the un-injured one. I have since then always slept on the right side of beds so that I can hang my right foot off the side when I sleep on my stomach.

By my senior year in high school, I had taken all the math and science offered at my school. I was enrolled in a special program through the Boy Scouts for those interested in medical vocations. Working in and around the hospital taught me some very important lessons. First and foremost, it showed me without a doubt that I did not want to be a doctor. I enjoyed the morgue best of all. The investigatory aspects of it brought out the former Agatha Christie fan that my father had fostered in me.

As I got closer to graduation, it became apparent that my mother's staunch opposition to my entering a religious order had not wavered. She was so excited about my going to college that I felt like I was on a runaway train. I had contacted several convents, and all of them turned me down. They didn't want a girl who was barely 18 without her parent's consent. I guess they didn't want to deal with runaways. My birthday that year was like so many of my other birthdays, almost unnoticed. It usually fell during Lent, which isn't a time of celebration.

The day I turned 18, and was officially an adult, I watched the evening news with horror that Archbishop Romero had been killed in San Salvador while saying mass. My Godmother took me to a memorial service at the Hispanic parish the next day. She said that being willing to die as a martyr is something she has always wondered if she would be able to do. You can never know until that moment if you will be able to choose death over giving up the faith.

Curveballs

I told her my dad had said something similar about never knowing if you can take a life until that moment is thrust upon you. With just two months left until my high school graduation, she told me that I had to finally accept the idea of honoring my mother's wishes. She knew I had dreams. We all have dreams that sometimes don't work out the way we planned. She showed me that there are many ways to serve without entering an order, and I was going to have to find my own path.

Chapter 5: Leaving Home

It was time for me to finally leave home. I had my scholarship and financing in place. All I had to do was pick a school and a major. Since it was not the path I really wanted to take, I decided to make the best of it, and to choose a major that would make me happy. I felt that if I could study something I was interested in, at a school that I was comfortable at, that I had the best chance of making decent grades. My mom wanted me to go to the college just to the south of us. I could even have commuted the 30 minutes to class. I knew I didn't want to go to that school under any circumstances. My choice was a safe 90 minutes away. My mother was just so pleased that I was going to college that she was willing to make the concession, besides, they had a great softball team, and that was my first love.

I picked Forestry as a major. I was once again surrounded by males. In my class there were 19 men and 5 women. All the professors were males. We also got to play with some serious toys. I loved it. I remember one Christmas telling my grandmother what I had been doing. She said that sounded like men's work, and gave me a very puzzled expression.

The transition to college was difficult in some respects, but I had been so independent for so long that there was no homesickness. I threw myself into my new classes. Learning to plant trees and run chain saws was much more interesting than my high school classes had been. When I found out that I could fulfill my physical education requirement with archery and riflery, I was delighted. The Riflery course was taught by a starchy sergeant first class. He was practically Rambo. It didn't take long for him to sign me up for the shooting team, and start pressuring me to join the ROTC program. I felt like I was trying one of everything in the smorgasbord of life.

I had dealt with military types before. I made such high grades in high school on the Armed Services Vocational Aptitude Battery tests, that I was followed every where I went my senior year by a couple of Marine recruiters. I could be in someone's back yard playing pick up basketball and they would miraculously appear.

Curveballs

Looking back, I think the reason I didn't join was because I didn't want to be a clerk. I would have wanted to be on the front line, and that was just not open to women at that time. Hanging out with some of the ROTC instructors in college allowed me to play with really cool toys.
 In both forestry and riflery, I was surrounded by men. I had been surrounded by men most of my life, so it seemed comfortable to me. The difference was that these men were also different. In high school, I either hung out with the female athletes, or with the math/science geeks. Neither put me in a position of serious dating. Those were safe places for me. I didn't want to date. I tried to protect myself completely from those things that other normal high schoolers did or talked about. In the locker room when the other girls would talk about things they were doing with their boy friends, I removed myself quickly from the conversation. The math nerds only talked about their latest science fair project. I did go on one date in high school towards the end.
 Mack was in all my math and science classes, and we had always competed against each other for the highest grade in our classes. We had been in the same homeroom every year of high school, even sharing a locker the last two. He was quiet and sweet. Towards the end of our senior year, he finally got up the nerve to ask me out to the end of school year carnival. I was so surprised that I accepted without thinking about the consequences. We had a very nice time. He didn't have a car, so I drove. I got to meet his mother instead of the other way around, and that suited me just fine. We held hands and walked down the midway playing some of the games. He even talked me into a Ferris wheel ride, and I hated rides.
 My first kiss had been years before with a neighborhood boy, but this good night kiss was my first real kiss, and it lasted about 10 seconds. It scared me. I almost felt overwhelmed by the feelings it brought up in me. I knew he was going out of state after high school, but we promised to keep in touch. His letters and calls were so sweet. He was homesick. He missed me. I didn't realize until then how much time we had spent

together over those 4 years. Eventually he admitted he wanted to marry me. I still wanted to be a nun. It was nice to be able to say I had a boyfriend even if he was far away, and even if I really didn't want to date. He was safe. Having a boyfriend also kept other guys at bay.

Early in my second semester I got a call that he had been in a wreck. He didn't make it. It was so far away that it didn't seem real. I had returned to my dorm after an afternoon working in the agronomy lab, and I found my roommate crying. I thought she had gotten bad news from home. When she told me she had taken the phone call about Mack's accident, I was numb. I felt so much guilt that he went to his grave thinking I would some day be his wife. Maybe I would have been. It was just another curveball thrown my way. When I finally started feeling again, I was determined to never let another man get that close to me.

I saw my roommates and friends continue to date, and I just couldn't bring myself to follow that course. There were even a few people who speculated that I must be a lesbian since I didn't date, and there were several lesbians in the forestry department. At times I would lie, just to keep people from asking uncomfortable questions, or looking at me funny. I may have not wanted to date, but I also didn't want to feel different from my friends. I wanted them to think I was worldly. I didn't want to feel left behind or left out. Twice a year the forestry department had a dance. They made me so uncomfortable. I ended up having to dance just to look and feel normal. I found someone safe though. Brian seemed as uncomfortable as I was. We never discussed why. Years later he became a priest, so I guess maybe I was safe for him too.

Chapter 6: The Second Surgery

I had originally injured my left knee shortly before having my ankle reconstructed. I knew I had the ankle surgery coming up, and I guess I was acting out a bit. I hurt it while doing a stupid stunt, showing off what a daredevil I am. That injury kind of got pushed to the back burner for my ankle. It came back to haunt me. All the walking I did in field work and around campus seemed to be taking a toll on my knee. My dream of playing spring softball evaporated. It didn't matter how far I could hit the ball, the coach said it would take a full time trainer to keep me on the field. My knee started locking up and swelling. I could no longer just ignore it. I finally broke down and went to the team doctor. His diagnosis was surgery. I still had nightmares about the rehab after my ankle surgery, but it had taken care of the problem. I had similar hopes for my knee surgery.

I waited until the summer after my freshman year. It was as horrible as I thought it was going to be. The worst part was that I could no longer run on my leg. I had been able to before the surgery even if it had been painful. The surgery that was supposed to help my knee actually made it worse. The surgery I had is no longer done for similar injuries. They stopped doing it about 2 years after I had my surgery done. If I had been able to wait, things might have been so different in my life. I don't know how it might have played out differently, but I would have had more options.

I struggled through the next three years of my forestry education favoring it. I tried not to let anyone know how much it was bothering me. I truly loved forestry. We had a logging competition team. How many women get to throw axes in college? I loved the atmosphere, the people I was around, and the coursework. It definitely fed my adrenaline addiction. I remember the summer we were in a swamp in South Carolina, and I had an extending metal pole 50 + feet up a tree when a lightening storm quickly moved in. Everyone should have a 50 foot long lightening rod in their hands at some point in their life. Waking up in a tent in the middle of a forest fire will also get your blood moving.

My knee continued to be like a shadow over everything. I should have had some rehab on it, but my insurance at the time would only pay for the surgery. Insurance was to be a stumbling block many times in my life. I slowed down, gained weight, and finally had to come to the realization that I was not going to be able to be a field forester. I didn't know what I was going to do.

I thought my only option was to go to graduate school and do research and teach. I was always told that those who could do things did them, and those who couldn't taught. I wanted to add some extra credits the summer before my senior year in college, so I decided to pick some classes that might make me more appealing to my preferred grad school. I signed up for a COBOL computer class and a class in Governmental budgeting. Neither of those classes had enough people sign up, so the computer assigned me randomly to another course in the business college in place of my cancelled computer class, and another course in the political science department for my cancelled government class. I ended up in Business Law and Administrative Law.

I was disappointed, but I needed the hours, and we had been told that business law can be helpful for foresters, so I decided to just take the classes. I was surprised. I found the classes very interesting, and I did very well. My business law professor was the faculty advisor to the pre-law club. He called me in for a conference. I thought I was in trouble. He asked me if I had ever considered attending law school. One of my forestry classmates a year ahead had just entered law school, so we had certainly all discussed it. I had also just been told that I would have trouble getting a posting in a forestry master's program because I was a woman. All these things weighed heavily on my mind. I decided to take the entrance exam. It was only $100 or so, and I decided that I would let that make the decision for me. My mother was so thrilled to hear I was considering law school, that she even paid for the testing.

My business law professor gave me information on some LSAT prep classes. I decided against them. First they were very expensive. Secondly, I wanted an accurate testing number. This test was supposed to gauge my ability to be successful in law school, and I didn't want any special information going in. So I showed up at the appointed time on a Saturday morning with my #2 pencils and my ID ready to test myself and my future. The test itself seemed to be mostly common sense or logic questions. I tried not to think about the results while waiting the weeks for the results to appear in my mailbox.

When I opened the envelope, and my grade said 42, I didn't think that was very good. It sounded like a failing grade to me. I took the results over to my professor, put them on his desk and asked it that would get me into a law school. He said, "It's not a matter of whether you can get in, it is a simple matter of where would you like to go?" He explained that a perfect score on the LSAT at that time was 46. In short order that grade coupled with my high grade point average had scholarship offers pouring in. My mother was ecstatic. I can't remember ever seeing her this pleased with me. I have to admit that felt very good. I truthfully believed that God was showing me the path he meant for me to take.

Of the offers I received, the one that really stood out was of all places Texas Tech. My mother wanted me to go to an Ivy League school. I didn't want to leave law school owing $100,000. I may have been able to work a couple of jobs most of the time while in college, but all the information the law schools were sending me made it clear that working even part time was frowned upon. They consider the study of the law to be a full time occupation. The premier school in Oklahoma was OU. That idea made me physically sick. I wanted to go to Texas Tech because it was an aggie school like I had come from. I thought I would be more comfortable there.

Texas Tech also had a program that would allow me to complete a master's degree in agricultural economics along with my law degree. I got some wonderful letters from the dean of the college encouraging me to attend. It reminded me a bit of when the Marine recruiters were following me around. Something though was nagging at me. My father had recently retired. He seemed to be failing. Something in the core of my being told me that I'd better stay a little closer to home. Against every bone in my body, I accepted OU's offer.

Curveballs

Chapter 7: Poison Ivy Walls

Law school is a hard place to be, especially when you really don't want to be there. Deep down inside, I quickly found that I did not want to be there. My initial enthusiasm was eroded almost immediately after meeting the people I was to spend the next 3 years with. The first strike against it was that it was at my alma mater's main rival. I didn't want to go anywhere near that hated school, but my University didn't have a law school. The second strike came when I realized what kind of education I was going to get. In my first semester, I was required to take a course on legal writing. It was designed to enable us to primarily write legal briefs. During the first class, the instructor informed us that the Oklahoma Supreme Court had just sent down an instruction to attorneys that all legal briefs from that time forward had to be limited to 10 pages or less. The professor told us for his class, to practice, all our briefs had to be 8 pages or less. My first brief was 7 ½ pages. I would have liked to have included more points, but I had to limit it to come in under the 8 page limit. I made a C- on the paper. I was satisfied because everyone I knew also made C's on the paper. This was a hard adjustment for most of us to make because everyone in my class had always been straight A students. For my next brief, I really knuckled down and hit every important point, and just did keep it to fewer than 8 pages. I made a C+. I was delighted at first. I felt like I was making progress in learning the craft. When I discovered that the professor had in fact given only one A+ on each of the first two papers, to the same student, who had written 20 and 24 page long briefs, I was livid. I learned my first hard lesson about the University of Oklahoma Law School. It was run on the do as I do system, not do as is written. They were training lawyers for the Good Ole Boy network, where winks and hand shakes were more important than following the rule of law. It disgusted me. The funny thing is, if I had felt a part of the place, I might well have left. Once I realized that they really didn't want me there, I was determined to stay.

Curveballs

I did everything that I could while in law school to expose the hypocrisy inbred there. I got into a public pissing match with the editor of the school newspaper about an article on acid rain. If an exam was scheduled for 3 hours, and I could finish it in one hour by not using complicated legalese language, and instead being clear and concise, I would do so. My classmates would moan when they saw me get up to turn in my exam book. I refused to buckle under to the pressure to conform. They were going to be so glad to get rid of me when I graduated.

Curveballs

Chapter 8: Fallen Hero

The summer before I began my final year of law school, my father began to really fail. I could just see it in his eyes. He had been seen at the VA Hospital in the spring, and they recommended that he have heart bypass surgery. My mother told him he couldn't have it, that he was too old. My father was starting to show the beginnings of dementia, and I think she was afraid of having to take care of him. We had a very hot summer. My brothers wouldn't bring their kids to visit, so my mother decided if she put in an above ground swimming pool, that the grandkids would want to come more often.

My job was to build a sun deck with stairs to make it easier for people to get into the pool. Early in the week, I remember driving onto our block, and seeing my father walk across the park. He stopped and leaned forward like he was trying to catch his breath. When I got to the house, my mom said he had pleurisy. He came in and sat in his chair with a heating pad on his chest. By Saturday, he was really uncomfortable. Mom decided to take him back to the VA. I knew that would be a long wait, so I decided to finish working on the deck. It was a scorching hot afternoon. Late in the day, one of our neighbors came into the back yard. She said my mother had been phoning. That my father had had a heart attack, and I needed to get to the hospital. I had loaned my car out, and didn't have a ride.

I called my Godmother. She had always come to my aid in an emergency. They were just on their way out the door to a formal dinner. So, I asked the neighbor lady who had brought me the news to drive me to the hospital. She was an older widow who drove very slowly. By the time I raced up the stairs at the hospital, they were wheeling my father into surgery. All he could do was reach out his hand as his gurney went past, and said, "I love you sweetie." After the swinging doors shut behind him, I saw my Godparents arrive. They had decided to skip their dinner to come sit with me. If it looked strange for a man in a Knights of Columbus tuxedo and a woman in a formal gown to be comforting a girl in dirty, sweaty work clothes, no one said anything.

When he came out of surgery later that night, they told us to go on home. It was late, and he seemed stable. I didn't even get to see him. I thanked my Godparents for sitting with me. I drove my mom and I home. As we walked in the door, the phone was ringing. It was the hospital telling us to return immediately. By the time we got there, he had already passed. He waited until I had left, I'm convinced, so that I wouldn't have to see him die. He also waited until a few minutes after midnight. That Saturday was one of my nephew's birthdays. I think he didn't want to die on his favorite grandson's birthday. My father was strong until the end, going out the best way he could.

The doctor's took us into a private room to tell us. I already knew. He had been given TPA which was part of a research project. He was only the second person in the state of Oklahoma to receive what was then an experimental drug, and is now the standard of care for not only heart attacks but also strokes. He had not benefited from it because they discovered during the autopsy that he had been having small heart attacks for several days. The clots had damaged too much of his heart muscle for the medicine to have a chance of saving him. What the autopsy also showed was that he did not have Alzheimer's disease. The dementia that he was experiencing was due to circulation problems that could have been helped by the heart bypass surgery the VA had recommended months before. In the core of my soul, for the rest of my life, I couldn't keep myself from blaming my mother for my father's death.

I spent the next several hours making arrangements and making phone calls. The next day we were supposed to go to the funeral home to make the arrangements. One brother was too far away to get here in time, another was having trouble with his wife and marriage. Another brother was having a different kind of problem with his wife. She wanted to know when the money from my father's estate would be distributed. I had to explain that everything went to my mother until she passed, so there would be no money going to anyone. My mother had basically fallen apart. What it meant practically, was that I had to make the arrangements for my father's funeral. I even had to write his obituary.

I remember walking through the display area with the undertaker. I knew my father would never have approved of me picking out an expensive one. A plain pine box would have made him very happy, but that was not an option for me. I finally settled on a simple, green metal one. He would have been happy that it was the cheapest one on the floor. My parents already had their burial plots paid for, and my father was receiving a free head stone because he was a veteran. I was in shock at how much everything else was costing. Even with all the large expenses already taken care of, his funeral cost $10,000. I would use this experience many times in the future when helping clients do their estate planning.

I went home to collect the clothing that the funeral director wanted. I got out my father's best suit. I had given it to him 3 years before at Christmas. He had never really had a nice suit before, and he had been going to a lot of funerals for his VFW friends. I wanted him to have something nice for a change. He wore it two years before to my college graduation. As I was pulling socks out of his drawer, I once again pulled out the familiar box that I used to look at as a child filled with my father's medals. When I put them back where I found them, I noticed some envelopes. I pulled out a stack that was several inches thick.

As I pulled cards out of the envelopes, I realized that my father had saved every card that my youngest brother Jimmy and I had ever given him. There were Father's Day cards, and birthday cards. There was even one of those Thanksgiving cards made out of construction paper where you trace the turkey out from around your hand. I separated out mine from Jimmy's. I put Jimmy's back in the drawer. After I took the clothing to the funeral home, they told me my father would be available for viewing in an hour. I came back and had the chapel to myself. It was the first time I had seen him since he had rolled past me in the hospital. I realized then that the last thing my father said to me was that he loved me.

I walked past his casket, and looked at his face. I reached into my bag, and pulled out the stack of cards I found in his drawer. I slid them into the inside pocket of his suit right above his heart. He had saved them for so many years, that I just wanted him to have them always. I was comforted by the thought that if sometime in the future someone finds my father, they may not know who he was, but they will understand that he was well loved.

That morning the sky opened, and it rained for the first time in many weeks. The Army sent an entire bus load of soldiers in dress uniforms to take care of the ceremony. My mother wanted the funeral to occur as quickly as possible. She wanted it on Monday morning. Many people later commented that they didn't get to come to the funeral because they didn't find out about it until the obituary was printed on Monday in the paper, and they read it too late to come. Even so, the chapel was full to standing room only. The military funeral was so solemn and impressive. It made me so proud to see these young men carry my father to his grave.

My first vocal teacher had come to sing the Ave Maria at the service. She had been called by the church, and didn't realize it was for my father until she arrived and saw me. She stood in the doorway to the chapel and couldn't come in as if she was frozen. I walked over to her, and took the music book from her hand when she started crying. I realized at that point that I hadn't cried yet for my father. I just looked at her. She said, "You look like you are holding up okay. How did it happen?" I told her his heart gave out, and that I thought I was still in a state of shock. She asked me if I wanted to sing with her. I said no. I didn't think I had it in me. I had sung at many funerals before and since, but I knew I couldn't sing for my father.

After the service, we went out to the grave site. He was to be buried under a tree. When the riflemen shot the volleys over his open grave, I was startled. One of my nieces began to cry out loud. I stood apart from my family. I hadn't really seen much of them since my father died. My Godparents stood on either side of me like pillars to hold me up incase I fell. My Godmother wept very quietly. My Godfather looked like he was biting down on his lip. I still could not cry. I watched the Army officer hand my mother the folded flag that had draped my father's casket. She seemed to be shaking so hard that my brother Jimmy took it from her.

    Then it was over. The soldiers loaded up in their bus, everyone started to drift away to their cars, and I just kept standing there staring at his grave and realized for the first time that I would never see my father again. I would never be able to call him with a problem, he would never get to walk me down the aisle if I married, he would never get to see my children, and he would never just be there like I had come to expect him to be. I don't know how long I stood there, but everyone had gone except my Godparents. Just like they had always been, they were there when I needed them. I feel to my knees, and buried my face in the wet grass, and finally cried for my father.

    My Godmother knelt down next to me, rubbed my back, and whispered to me that it was okay to cry. She said to cry for myself, but not to cry for my dad. She told me that no matter what his short comings might have been, he was a good man, and a good father, and that I would see him again one day. She said that she promised me that I would see him, because Christ had promised us. I looked up at her, and asked, "Why did he have to leave me alone?" She pulled me to her chest, rocked me like she had so many times when I was young, and told me that I would never be alone, that they would be there for me as long as I needed them. My Godfather helped me to my feet, and gave me a ride back to my mother's house. For some reason, it would never again feel like my home.

Chapter 9: Sleep Walking

Two weeks later I was back at law school for my final year. I think I sleepwalked through the entire year. I'm not sure how I kept from flunking out. The people around me seemed so wooden. It was almost as if my world had lost all color, and everything was in black and white. The only thing I put any passion into was an essay for an environmental competition put on by the Association of Trial Lawyers. I won much to my surprise. I was to receive a national award from the Dean of the college at our convocation. I chose not to go. It was my final slap at the establishment of the University. I think they were quite happy to be rid of me.

Those first steps out of the academic arena into the real world can be very scary. I was in law school, preparing to be a lawyer, yet had no idea what I was going to do as a lawyer. I knew that I didn't want to practice personal injury law. I didn't want to end up in a small cubical in a large firm with no chance of advancement. Then a unique opening came up, and they were looking for new graduates with backgrounds in Agriculture. The only other student in my class that had a bachelor's degree in Agriculture was headed to work in his father's law firm, so I kind of got the job by default.

In the middle 80's, a graduate student in the Agriculture Engineering department decided to do a state review of the death certificates of farmers. He was trying to find something to do his masters thesis on, and thought that perhaps he could find a common link to some type of farm equipment that was so dangerous it was killing farmers so that he could redesign it to make it safer. What his project showed instead is that, by far, the leading cause of death among farmers in Oklahoma during that time period was suicide. The powers that be, in the staunchly conservative Bible belt district that is Oklahoma, freaked out.

Farmers and ranchers have always been viewed as the backbone of Oklahoma's economy and culture. That so many were committing suicide was like some kind of collective shame on the state. The State Department of Agriculture decided to try to throw some money at the issue. The problem was in trying to figure out what they could do to help. Farmers in that part of the world do not trust the government. So they figured the best way to handle the situation was to find an organization that the farmers would trust enough to turn to for help. That organization ended up being the Oklahoma Council of Churches.

By the time I was brought on board, the OCC had set up a toll free hot-line to allow farmers or their families to call in to talk to a counselor. That line was manned by the widow of a farmer who had died of a heart attack after losing the family farm. She was a qualified counselor who had worked as a high school guidance counselor and eventually school principal. The other counselor on staff coordinated regional support groups. Farmers are very independent souls who do not ask for help easily. The hotline and support groups were basically triage. Once they had stopped the bleeding, they needed to move beyond to help the farmers fix the problems that led to the desperation and depression in the first place.

It did seem strange to have a law practice where I rarely saw my clients. With access to a toll-free hotline with a free lawyer at the other end, I spent large amounts of time giving legal advice over the phone to disembodied voices. This was where my insistence on never speaking in legalese came in handy. I was able to explain to these very simple, but not unintelligent, men complicated legal issues. You have to be very careful dealing with these kinds of strong willed men. I couldn't talk down to them, and I couldn't talk over their heads. I had one rule that I always stuck to—if I didn't know something, I told them so, but always promised to find out the answer. I found out quite quickly that farmers had all the same problems that regular people have including divorces and probate and the occasional criminal case. I had to practice a general practice one minute, and complicated loan restructuring and tax issues the next.

Being the only attorney in the organization meant that I was called on to do a variety of other duties. That is often the case when working for a non-profit organization. We were an umbrella organization for a refugee resettlement program, crop walk, disaster recovery, and a seemingly unending list of smaller ecumenical duties. One day I might be sorting out donated can goods, and the next day trying to settle a dispute between a local church's pastor and board of deacons. Once a year we would put on a Day at the Legislature for religious organizations where we explained to them which bills before the legislature that year might be of interest to them, and how to lobby the people involved with the legislation. I had to learn to be a real lawyer on the job with literally no help from a more experienced attorney. There was another thing that I had to learn on my own, how to deal with my own money.

Curveballs

Chapter 10: Jumping The Bar

My first court appearance was just a month after I was admitted to the Bar. There was a 12 year old girl who needed open heart surgery that her parents wouldn't consent to because they were Jehovah Witnesses. The parents and the doctors both had attorneys representing them. The judge decided that the girl should be represented as well. Since Legal Aid was representing the parents, they could not represent the girl. The judge asked the Legal Aid attorney if he knew of anyone available that could quickly be brought up to speed. Legal Aid's offices were one floor below our office. He mentioned to the judge that the Council had a new attorney. He apparently didn't know how new.

The judge thought having a "church lawyer" made a lot of sense considering the case specifics. I received a call from the judge's clerk to come in. It scared me. I thought I had done something wrong like sign my Bar card in the wrong place. I quickly told the director I had to go see a judge. He also wanted to know what I had done wrong. I flew down the front marble staircase and ran to my car.

I didn't even know where to park when I got there. It took me a half an hour to even find his office. I don't know what I expected a judge's chambers to look like, but this one reminded me of a principal's office. He introduced himself and explained what he wanted from me. Then he asked, "You look pretty young, when were you admitted to the Bar?" When I told him that I'd only had my license a month, he audibly exhaled, and said, "Well, you might as well hit the ground running. This is one of those cases where we have to do everything right because it will probably be appealed. Do your homework, and ask for help if you need it. Other than that, it is basically the same as Moot Court from law school. Good luck."

With that he stood up, shook my hand, and I was dismissed. As I walked out the door, his clerk had a pile of folders to hand me. He informed me I would receive $40/day and parking. I had him explain about the parking, and also had him show me where the courtroom was going to be. I had a week to prepare a case full of constitutional issues, and expert medical testimony. As I was leaving the courthouse, it dawned on me that I didn't even own a dress.

I called my mom in a panic when I got back to the office. I needed her to do my hair, and I needed to borrow a dress. I had borrowed dresses from her before in college, for the weddings of my friends, or a dance, even for my Moot Court appearance. She knew something was up, but I didn't tell her what because I was afraid that she'd show up to watch, and I'd be too nervous to perform.

She loaned me the same dress she always did. It was the only one she had that was long enough for me. She was 7-8 inches shorter than I was. I preferred dresses that went well below my knee. I told myself that it was modesty, but it was actually vanity. I hated having people gawk at the foot long scar on my left knee.

I threw myself into the issues behind the case to the point that they had to throw me out of the law library at the court house when it closed. I basically had no conception of time and was barely sleeping. I finally felt like I had the entire file memorized and all cases even remotely on point, briefed. I put a stop to the research to get a really good night's sleep the night before my appearance.

I was so nervous. I got to court an hour early and had to sit and wait. When the case was finally called, I almost jumped through my skin, but once I took my place behind the podium, I felt a calm come over me. I presented my arguments, and was asked a few questions of clarification from the judge. My opponent from Legal Aid took his turn. I was allowed rebuttal where I really made my strongest argument that a person has the complete right to religious belief, but not to religious practice. If the parent's religious belief's included human sacrifice, we would not be in court debating it. When I made the argument that this little girl's parent's right to their religious beliefs end where their little girl's right to live begins. The judge started crying. I didn't expect that. I wasn't sure if that was a good sign or not.

I won. It felt like sinking a shot at the buzzer or hitting a home run in the bottom of the ninth inning. It

Curveballs

felt great. Her parents came up to me in the corridor, and thanked me. They felt they had to contest the surgery even if they actually wanted her to have it. My opponent took me down the street to a bar. It was "The" Lawyer's Bar, and I was required to buy a round for the house to celebrate my first court victory. I didn't mind the $600 bill on my credit card at all. The judge even came up to me later that evening. He was quite intoxicated, and slapped me on the back. His only comment was "You're welcome in my court anytime, counselor."

Chapter 11: The Escalator

After that first trip to court, I was eager to go again. I started looking for other cases to take, other hurdles. I wanted as many challenges as possible. I tried to keep myself as busy as possible in the evenings. I think this was my way of staying so occupied that I didn't have time to think about things I was trying to avoid. I volunteered at a mental health clinic, a homeless shelter, and served on a variety of committees at church in addition to the theology classes I was taking once a week. I spent a lot of my free time helping people caught up in the beginnings of the AIDS epidemic. They often lost their jobs, their homes, and their families, so they ended up at the homeless shelter. I fought to help them get their disability benefits so that they could get some treatment, and a place to live. For some, by the time I could get them the money they needed to get their own places, they were ready for the hospice instead.

Many of my clients at the homeless shelter who didn't have AIDS were mentally ill. The mentally ill make up such a large percentage of the homeless population, and they are traditionally so much harder to house. These cases taught me a lot about estate planning and disabilities. They also brought me a financial independence that I had never known before. It seems strange to say that I made more money representing homeless, disabled individuals at night and on my lunch hour than I did with my day job. Many AIDS patients were homeless because of alienation, not lack of finances, and the way the disability rules were written, those who received their benefits were paid a lump sum dating back to the last day they worked, with 20% of the lump sum going to their attorney.

I would like to be able to say that I donated all my fees right back to the homeless shelter. I didn't. I volunteered so many hours doing routine things for people that couldn't afford to pay anything, that I felt like the fees I did get paid, I deserved. I had grown up poor, and never had this much money thrown at me all at once before. I didn't know what to do with it. The last two years of law school had especially been difficult financially because I didn't have my scholarship renewed after the first year. I started by increasing my contributions to the church and other charities. I began taking night school theology classes, and traveling. I also started eating better. I had really neglected my health in college, and especially after my father died. I recognize now that I had been in a depression brought on by the grief.

A better diet and a weight loss gave me a new perspective on life. I woke up one day and realized that I was actually happy. I hadn't been in a long time. I started taking up old forgotten hobbies. I began singing and volunteering at church. I started playing basketball again. I joined the church softball team. I even began jogging again. Somewhere along the way, my knee had gotten better. Maybe it was just a matter of time for it to heal more fully. It didn't like the increased wear and tear though. Sometimes I would come up hobbling, but slogged through it.

I also took a lot of pride in the job I doing. Just because I hadn't really wanted to be a lawyer didn't make me a bad one. When I started giving public speeches and going to court regularly, I realized I needed a better wardrobe. My mother and I had always sewn most of my dress clothes. I never really put much thought into clothing before. My new financial situation really opened some windows for me. I was able to buy my first new car. I bought a house. I invested in things like really expensive musical instruments, custom leather shoes, and an extensive wardrobe. I had grown up with my mother doing my hair, and reveled in being able to go to a real hair salon.

I paid a fashion consultant to go shopping with me. She took me to Dallas and introduced me to clothes by Dior, Gucci, Chanel, and Armani. When I found a pair of shoes that I liked, I bought 4 pairs in different colors. My favorite briefcase was a Ferragamo that matched the shoes I had custom made for court appearances. My court suits were tailored Armani. It made me feel important. It made me feel grownup and independent. My mother finally got to see me in dresses again. My frugal father would have been horrified. I thought I was just living life to the fullest, but looking back, it seemed as if I was trying to fill an emptiness in my life with material things, and the excitement of litigation.

The courtroom excited me in a way that nothing else ever had. I had played sports, and won championships. I was fiercely competitive. I took risks. I thought nothing of going backpacking by myself at the age of 16. I used to terrorize a former roommate with my rock climbing. She would pace beneath me on the ground pleading with me to please not go any higher. Running chain saws didn't scare me; forest fires didn't scare me, and even wandering around in foreign countries by myself, didn't scare me. The adrenaline of ripping apart a witness on the witness stand was intoxicating. I was like a predator. It got to the point where people did not want to face me in court. That took some of my fun away. It was as if I needed to find a new prey to satisfy my hunger.

Chapter 12: Finding New Prey

When trying to keep a farmer on his farm, there might have been a dozen or more creditors to deal with. Some were from government agencies, state and federal, some were quasi-governmental banks, local banks, equipment dealers, feed and seed stores, and sometimes doctors, lawyers and even family members. I quickly discovered that some of the financial problems that my farmers had, had nothing to do with their farms. Whenever there are desperate people, there are always those who are willing to take advantage of the situation.

When I was dealing with a farmer whose grandfather had maintained the homestead through the dust bowl and depression, and whose father had kept it together during the war, it was so hard to explain to them why they couldn't hold onto the farm now. Sometimes the only way to save a farmer was for him to lose the farm. I could try to explain about the economics of international trade and price supports, but it just didn't make any sense to them. So when the snake oil salesmen came to town explaining to them that their troubles were because of an international Jewish banker conspiracy backed by the US government, they latched on to that explanation. That made sense to them.

My dad always told me that the best way to deal with bad guys is to learn everything you can about them. When one of my farmers would call me with information about one of these rural meetings, instead of just telling them to stay clear of those guys, I began to ask them to take me to the meetings with them. These men were telling distressed farmers that they could save their farms by paying off their mortgages and debts with sight drafts.

Basically they were trying to sell farmers a package of essentially worthless financial documents drawn on fictitious banks. They would use these checks to pay off their mortgages, and by the time the paperwork made its way through the financial network, and was discovered to not be legitimate, the bank had usually already released the mortgage. That meant there was a mess to clean up legally. In some cases the farmers had taken out loans from family members to pay for the packages, and had begun to make monthly mortgage payments to these fraud artists.

Even worse, since it was the farmer's name on the documents, not the fraud artists, it was the farmers who were on the hook for any criminal charges due to the bank fraud. I could usually talk a farmer out of falling into this trap by letting them talk to a farmer that had been destroyed by this scheme. The farmers who didn't come to me until after they had been taken advantage of still haunt me. I knew these guys needed to be stopped. I had found my new prey.

I began going to every one of their rural sale's pitches. I collected all the information on them I could, including secretly taping conversations with as many of the different individuals as possible. I began to notice other men coming to all the meetings. They reminded me of the posse that used to follow our high school football quarterback around. They were all kind of big and dumb, but looked very menacing.

About 3 months into my investigations, I finally got a close look at their "quarterback." He was this kind of short, slight, middle-aged man, who had one of those near permanent tans that you knew belonged to someone who spent all their time working outside. I couldn't get close to him for several weeks. He showed up at one meeting in army fatigues. I didn't think anything about it at first, because camouflage clothing is common in rural Oklahoma. When I got a little closer to him, I realized that his was actually a uniform. It showed him to be a lieutenant colonel in the Oklahoma Air National Guard. That really confused me. I finally was able to find out that he had been a pilot in the Air Force in Vietnam, and remained in the reserves after coming home. I also found out that not only was he promoting these worthless sight drafts, he had used one himself to try to save his farm from foreclosure. As soon as the government had sued him, he filed bankruptcy to further complicate and delay his foreclosure.

This man was dangerous. That I knew without having to be told. When dealing with con artists, I knew that they were basically only interested in the money or the power. This man though, was a true believer. He wasn't Göring, he was Goebbels. I knew I had to be careful, but I also knew that I had to get closer to him. At one of the weekly meetings, I saw him talking to a farmer I knew. This farmer wasn't really one of my clients, but I had met him at the office many times because he had been a close friend to our counselor's deceased husband. Our in house counselor was a nice enough woman, but she was so hard core about keeping every farmer on their land, she wouldn't compromise even when it was in the farmer's best interest. I tended to deal with her at arm's length. Now, I knew I had to use her to get what I wanted.

Chapter 13: Putting on a Mask

I used our counselor to get close to this farmer who was close to the man I wanted to meet. After several weeks, I was finally successful. I felt like I was being followed. Turns out I was right. One weekend, while I was standing under a shade tree on a particularly hot afternoon, the Colonel walked up to me and started a conversation about football. In Oklahoma, football is close to a religion. In a way, I think he was checking me out. I had all the right answers. He probed me about many things that afternoon, politics, farming, and even my knowledge of military history. My father had seen to my education in the latter. He seemed content with my answers. He told me he had a place in the country that he liked to go to on Saturday afternoons that had a nice gun range. He wondered if I had kept up my riflery skills after leaving school. I hadn't mentioned that I had been on the rifle team. That's the first moment that I really had a sense of fear. I realized that he had been investigating me even before he had approached me.

I inhaled deeply trying not to let my fear be evident. If I showed any fear, it might put me into more danger. I told him that I looked for any opportunity to use my target rifle. He invited me to join him in two weeks. We made the arrangements, and he excused himself to mingle with the rest of the crowd. I was left alone with my thoughts. It is so hard to know where fear ends and excitement begins. I knew I had my work cut out for me over the next two weeks. The first thing I had to do was actually buy a target rifle.

The rifles I had used in college had been supplied by the college's ROTC department, and the range had been underneath the football stadium. I had access to neither anymore. Monday during my lunch hour I drove to the closest sporting goods store, and walked up to the gun counter. I felt as if I was doing something quite illicit. I was afraid that I would be seen by someone who knew me. When the clerk came over, I told him that I was looking for a target rifle. He tried to show me a large hunting rifle. I told him that I was more interested in a .22 caliber. He looked at me as if I had just passed gas. He informed me that he had some kid sized weapons that were .22 caliber. I realized that I was in trouble. If a clerk looked down on me, what would these hard core ex-military types think? I decided that if I was going to pass myself off as one of them, I'd better start acting the part quickly. I chuckled slightly, and then whispered to the clerk that I would need something better than a kid's rifle. He looked impatient, and asked what kind of rifle I had used before. I explained about being on the rifle team in college, and his demeanor changed a bit. I told him that I wanted a .22 because I planned to put a lot of rounds through it, and .22s where just cheaper. He started to warm to me. He said, "So you are looking for a high capacity .22, that's different." He went past the row of cabinets with glass doors containing many different types of hunting rifles and shotguns to a cabinet with a solid door. When he finally found the proper key to open it, it revealed an array of military style weapons. Some I had fired for familiarization in college, but some I had only seen in movies like Rambo.

He pulled out a rifle with a folding stock and a long banana clip. He handed it to me. It was a Ruger 10/22. My eyes must have shown because it was love at first sight. The clerk just nodded knowing that he was going to get his commission out of me. I had always loved rifles. I had grown up around hunters, but always refused to go myself. I could never bring myself to kill an animal. I couldn't wait for the summer after 7th grade when I was finally going to be old enough to take riflery in summer camp. I had steady hands, and a real desire to be a good shot, and I was. I was the only girl on the team my freshman year in college, but had never owned my own rifle. I found myself running my hands over the weapon, and peering down the sight.

Now that the clerk knew that I was going to buy the rifle, he started stacking other things up on the counter. A stack of large capacity ammo clips, my choice of slings and cases, and a variety of items that I had never seen before, appeared magically before my eyes. I made my selections based on what I thought a regular shooter would have acquired over several years. I had to look the part. At least that is what I told myself. I recognize now that I was also very drawn towards this type of lifestyle. When I had finally decided on my accessories, and the clerk totaled everything up, it was more than my mortgage payment. The clerk looked concerned for a moment that the price might cause me to reconsider, but was relieved when I casually plunked down my credit card.

I paid for everything but the large amount of ammunition I had picked out. I could buy any amount of armament I wanted, but I couldn't buy ammo for it at the same time. I actually had to be escorted outside to lock the new rifle in my car, and then return to purchase the ammo separately. I am still stunned to this day that I was able to purchase a semi-automatic weapon, with 30 round clips and all the ammo I could carry so easily and so quickly. I left with plenty of time to still have lunch and make it back to the office on time.

I'm embarrassed to admit that I couldn't concentrate on my work for the rest of the afternoon. I spent it calling around to shooting ranges trying to find the ideal place to try out my new toy. I kept going to the window to look outside to make sure that no one had broken into my car. I finally just gave up and left work early. When I pulled into the driveway, I actually checked both directions to make sure none of the neighbors where watching me carry all the packages inside.

I couldn't wait to tear into the box and pull my new rifle out. I must have spent an hour cleaning and oiling it. I installed the replacement stock. It had come with a standard wood stock, but I had gotten a folding stock just like the display model had. I toyed with the sling forever to get it adjusted just the way I wanted it. The gun case looked too new. I had purposefully not bought a new gadget case for my extra gear because of that very reason. I had an old camera gadget bag that I knew had just the right look of use and even misuse. I didn't have anything remotely similar that could house my rifle. I did the only thing I could think to do. I took it outside and stomped it into the ground.

My next door neighbor came out on his back porch. If he thought there was anything strange going on, he didn't let on, but he did go back inside quickly after putting some fresh food out for his dog. My dog was having too much fun to bark at our neighbor, which he normally did every time the man moved. Buster thought my rifle case was a new play toy. He loved to dig, so if I was playing in the dirt, I must have meant for him to play too. He actually grabbed a hold of the narrow part of the nylon case, and proceeded to take off with it across the yard. I gave chase, but he disappeared under the house with it. I had crawled under the house many times to retrieve things that crazy basset decided needed to be hoarded or buried, but this had to be the strangest.

I didn't have the time for our ordinary tug of war, so I went into the house, grabbed a box of dog biscuits to keep him occupied, and did my best army crawl to retrieve my new rifle case. At the end, I decided the dog did me a favor. The case looked like it had done rough duty. His teeth marks left a hole that could have even passed for a bullet hole. I felt I was ready to blend in. I thought about trying to make the rifle looked as world worn, but decided against it. I just couldn't bring myself to damage it. That turned out to be a wise decision.

I had an appointment at the gun range at 7pm that evening. I spent the rest of my time loading ammo into clips. I still ended up getting to the range almost an hour early in my excitement. I wondered how I was ever going to be able to steady my heartbeat enough to hit the target. I was planning to put as many rounds through my new rifle as possible during the time I had before my afternoon with the Colonel. I made appointments for every night that week except for Wednesday when my theology class met. I decided that the most important thing was to properly zero my new toy, and get very comfortable with it. I needed to look as if I had been shooting regularly for years.

When my time finally came up, I was escorted to my cubicle. The range was in the basement under an old bowling alley. Each station had a counter top with a shelf, and a bar stool. I unzipped my rifle from its case and placed it in the gun rest. The first thing I removed from my gadget bag was my hearing protection. The noise in the basement was already deafening. Even with these head phone like protectors over my ears, I still felt uncomfortable. I dug around in my bag for a pair of those foam rubber ear plugs that had come as a free gift with my rifle. With those in my ears, and the larger headphones over them, I finally felt that I had the silence I would need to concentrate. Next I put on a pair of safety glasses. Once I had both in place, the shooting range assistant looked me over, nodded, and went about his business.

I saw a stack of paper targets on the shelf in my cubicle. I pulled one out, clipped it onto the track in front of me, and then hit the switch on the wall to my left. The target zipped quickly down the range until it stopped. I grabbed a full clip of ammo, slid it into place with a silent snap, and tried in vain to still my racing heart. I decided that I should just begin to fire, and worry about precision after I had broken the barrel in. I made the familiar motion of sliding the sling across the back of my left hand, and gently raised the rifle to seat it against my right shoulder. The trigger was quite stiff. After what seemed an eternity, I finally felt the trigger give way. The recoil wasn't as hard as I had expected. I had hit the third ring. Not bad for a first shot through a new rifle after a lay off of 8 years.

Before the evening was over, I had expended an entire brick of .22 ammunition. Normally I would have immediately cleaned my weapon, but decided to carry it home smelling of gun powder to "season" my gun case. When I got home, I dutifully cleaned and oiled it before putting the trigger lock back on and sliding it under my bed. In the next 10 days I think I put more rounds through that rifle than I did in an entire season with the riflery team. By the time I packed it in my trunk to make the drive to the country, I was comfortable enough with my new rifle that I hoped I would be able to pass myself off as a regular shooter. My life might depend on it.

Curveballs

Chapter 14: Going to the Country

    I woke early that morning, after a fitful night's sleep. I kept waking up afraid I had overslept. I put a lot of thought into what I was going to wear. I had an old pair of army fatigues that had belonged to one of my brothers in the closet that I used when working in the garden. I thought about wearing those, but decided to go more as I would to a church picnic. I pulled a pair of Levi's 501's out. I had worn those kinds of jeans since high school. I would be most comfortable in them, and I might really need that comfort before the day was over. I put a thermal underwear shirt on with an old t-shirt over that. I often thought of that as my forester uniform. I had spent many days in the woods dressed like that.
    In my nervousness, I spent the most time deciding on which shoes to wear. I didn't own a pair of cowboy boots, and hadn't since I was a kid. I had a pair of old steel-toed logging boots somewhere in the back of my closet, but only dug them out when I was running a chain saw, mostly out of habit. I would normally wear my Nike light hiking boots, but was afraid they might think that wasn't "country" enough. I stopped myself. I was over thinking. I didn't want to look like I was trying too hard to fit in, so I wore what was comfortable, my hiking boots were it. I actually thought about changing the shoelaces out. I had always removed the shoelaces that come with my boots and replaced them with a bright color. Everyone has to have a "thing." I finally decided to leave the bright red laces. I just hoped I wasn't making a mistake.
    It was such a pretty day, and a nice drive. I tried to stay as relaxed as possible. I put a tape of familiar music in the stereo, and sang really loudly along with it. The trip seemed almost too short. I tried to think of answers that I could give to a variety of questions. I knew that whenever possible, I should tell the complete truth. Besides being the easiest to remember, I was less likely to get confused. I also decided to try to keep in check my natural propensity to talk non-stop. Out of everything, that would probably prove to be most difficult. I thought for my own safety, silence, or discretion would have to be my companion. I would

Curveballs

have no other. I was entering bare and without a safety net.

I stopped at a country store, and went in. I dug in my pocket for the phone number I was supposed to call. The quarter hit the floor twice because my hands were shaking so hard. The man who answered the phone was cautious, but said that he would send someone in about 15 minutes to escort me in. I walked over to the cooler, and started to grab a coke. I thought better of it. The last thing I needed was a caffeine rush. I settled for a sprite, paid the clerk, and waited on the porch. There were two older men sitting on an old park bench out front. They barely acknowledged my presence. I understood these kinds of folks. They don't like outsiders.

After what seemed like a very long 15 minutes, an old green pickup truck drove into the gravel parking lot. A medium height man with sandy blonde hair stuck his head out the window, and told me to follow him. He had an accent that I couldn't quite place. It sounded kind of German, but not quite. As I was getting back into my car, the men on the porch that had ignored me before, looked at me with a renewed interest. They obviously knew this truck, or the man driving it. I followed him across a small bridge over a very red creek, down a dirt road, and then across a cattle grate and through a large metal gate that was promptly closed behind us. The sound of that gate closing made my heart start racing again.

I parked surrounded by an assortment of SUV's and old trucks. I saw the Colonel coming down the steps of an old farm house. I walked over to him, and shook his hand. He asked the usual stuff, did I have a nice drive, did I find the place easily, etc. He was definitely trying to put me at ease. I practically felt like I was being buttered up for something. He took me inside the house. In what should have been the front parlor was a row of filing cabinets with a desk in front of them. It reminded me of an army day room. He took me back to the kitchen, and offered me some coffee. I settled for some lemonade. It was way too sweet, but I didn't say anything. There was a large plate of donuts on the table, and an assortment of coffee cups. Again, it looked

like the same white china cups that every army officer's mess contained. I wondered where all of the men were who had been drinking coffee there. Except for the Colonel and the man who had led me out to the farm, I hadn't seen any other people, the full parking lot not withstanding.
    It was as if everything was being carefully orchestrated for my visit. I was starting to feel a bit like a puppet, and I wondered what the puppet master was going to require of me. I heard the Colonel talking softly to someone towards the back of the house, and then he returned to the kitchen, poured himself a cup of coffee, and sat at the table with me. I knew that everything that I said from that point forward would be so important. I had to be very careful. I also needed to take in every sight and sound I heard.
    He asked me some general questions about my background and my family. He seemed to be most interested in my father and my brothers' military service. He liked the fact that I had joined the VFW Auxiliary. He seemed to be testing the waters on my political ideals. He asked about why my youngest brother hadn't gone into the service. This was the first question that I had to really think about. I decided the complete truth might be the best way to handle this. I told him that my brother's 18th birthday fell right after the draft ended in '75, but that before that, my dad had told him that if he got drafted, if he wanted to go to Canada, that my dad would support him in the decision. He asked if my dad had made the same offer to my older brothers who all served, and I said no, that as the war had dragged on; my dad had become disillusioned with the government's handling of the war, and could no longer support it. That explanation really seemed to brighten the Colonel's face.
    He asked me if I wanted to see the rest of the farm. I felt like I had passed some sort of initiation test. I followed him out the kitchen door onto an old sleeping porch that had an army cot, a storage locker with some pretty substantial locks, and a large book shelf filled with dog-eared manuals, and stacks of dusty books. I noticed a pair of binoculars on the small table next to the cot, and decided they probably weren't for bird watching. We walked down a set of pre-cast concrete steps, and

out into the shade of a rather large elm tree. There must have been over a dozen picnic tables scattered around in the shade.

As he pointed out various small buildings, I couldn't help but notice that I was seeing no actual farm equipment. Each had a name and a function. Most of the buildings were for various types of storage. It seemed like he was storing a considerable amount of food. We walked through a large Quonset hut that had an impressive machine shop. It reminded me of the shop at my brother, John's truck repair facility, with a few differences. I had never seen one up close, but had seen one in a magazine before, and I was pretty sure that I was looking at an ammunition reloading machine. I inhaled deeply, and could smell gunpowder and gun oil. I had smelt both quite a bit in the last two weeks. It looked to me like a large gun-smithing operation. I tried to pretend like I either didn't see anything interesting, or that I just didn't know what I was looking at. Sometimes being a woman who isn't supposed to know about male stuff can come in handy.

We went out the back door of the Quonset hut, and I was pretty sure that I saw movement out of the corner of my eye in the trees. I got the feeling that I was being watched again. There was a large grassy area right behind the hut that was surrounded on three sides by a typical Oklahoma scrub pine/oak mix. Even in spring time the leaves were brown. The grassy area seemed to have a natural depression in the middle that had a fire ring. It reminded me of the large council fire rings at my Camp Fire Girls summer camp. It was obvious to me that this area had a special function. He seemed to actually walk around it reverently as if it was holy ground.

Our next stop was the shooting range. It was in a hollow where the backdrop was the far bank of a small dry creek bed. The shooting positions all seemed to be in covered places. Some were behind hay bales, or particle board lean-tos. The only thing I could think of at the time, was wondering where his actual fields were. I hadn't seen a chicken, a cow, or a stalk of wheat or corn. It was beginning to dawn on me that this was a farm in name only. It was as if it hit me all at once that I had

Curveballs

walked into, talked myself into a place I had no business being. I had a cold chill go up my spine, and had another wave of fear come over me.

Chapter 15: A Walk in the Park

When we finished touring the grounds, we walked back towards the farm house. I still had not seen any other people. I knew there were other people on the property. I could hear gun fire in the distance. I could hear the sound of car engines and doors. It seemed as if everyone was going out of their way to avoid me, or just to avoid being seen. We went back through the back door of the farm house, into the kitchen. While we had been gone, someone had come in and started cooking, but they had also disappeared. There was a large pot of chili on the stove, and it seemed as if something was being cooked in the oven as well.

He motioned for me to sit down at the table, and went into the other room. I heard him talking to the man that had come to get me. The next thing I knew, the kitchen was filled with people and activity. It was like someone turning on a light switch. A woman and a man came in and started attending to the cooking, and a half a dozen other men, most dressed in fatigues came in and sat at the large dining table. They were all seemingly in the middle of conversations, and continued as if I wasn't even there. I sat there about 15 minutes trying to listen to all the conversations going on. Some were ordinary about a game they had seen on TV or something their girlfriends had done. A few were talking about more interesting things. Two men at the end of the table were talking about some kind of delivery they were expecting, and had been delayed by customs. I couldn't quite hear or figure out what the delivery contained.

The cooks started ladling out chili, and placed a large bowl of fresh biscuits in the middle of the table. I'd had better of both at my mom's table, but they were passable. Everyone else was eating like it was their last meal. The talking almost all disappeared. After lunch, the Colonel and two of the men we had lunch with escorted me out to my car to retrieve my rifle. We walked down to the firing range which was now full of activity.

There were a lot of men and women on the gun range who had not been with us at lunch. They were all dressed in camouflage army fatigues. Some were wearing berets, and some where wearing old style army helmets. One actually had a helmet on with twigs and branches attached to the top like in an old war movie. If it hadn't been so scary, I might have laughed out loud. They looked silly, like 10 year olds playing army in someone's back yard. What I had to keep reminding myself is that these people weren't playing, and nothing they were doing was funny.

    I watched the other shooters for a few minutes while the Colonel looked over my rifle. I saw him messing with the action and dry firing it. He turned to me and said he just wanted to make sure that my weapon was clean and safe. He said that it appeared ship shape and well loved. I was hoping that he hadn't noticed that the weapon was still pretty new, although I had put enough rounds through it to wear a patina in the bluing on the barrel. About the time he was finished looking at my rifle, the man in the helmet with twigs attached, stood up and barked orders at the rest of the people on the firing range. They all jumped up, got into lines, and marched off on his command. I was stunned. It was as if I was watching an army basic training unit.

    After the troops had marched out to wherever they were headed, the Colonel motioned me into a firing position. It was about 100 yards from the embankment where the targets were attached. He said we had about 20 minutes before the next unit came through. I wondered how many "units" he had on the property at that moment. I knew I was being recruited and handled with kid gloves at the same time. I just hoped I could make a good showing on the range as nervous as I was feeling.

    I decided since my best shooting position had always been the prone position, that I had better go with that. I sat on the ground behind the firing position. I opened up my gadget bag and removed my eye and ear protection. I debated for a second about which clip of ammunition to pull out. The standard clip was small and held only 10 rounds. I had several, but found it was more convenient to use a larger capacity clip. I had several 30 round clips, and pulled one of those out. I could see the Colonel's head nod slightly. He approved of my having high capacity clips. It was obvious to me that everything I did or said was being evaluated.

He said, "I noticed that your rifle is drilled for a sight, but you don't use one." I replied, "I used to use a scope, but found it limited my field of vision, and ability to react to quickly changing situations. At that response, his mouth cracked a half smile. So far I seemed to be saying the right things. I had to be careful that it didn't seem that I was only saying things that he wanted to hear. I put on some shooting gloves and a shoulder pad. He raised an eyebrow at that. He asked me if I had trouble with kickback. I explained that kickback didn't bother me, but I was nervous and wanted to deaden any extra vibration so it didn't transfer to the trigger. He seemed to nod his head slightly. Admitting I was nervous was important at that point, and showing that I knew how to prevent it from affecting my shooting seemed to make a good impression as well.

In all, I went through about 100 rounds. I tried a variety of shooting stances and positions all over the range. Always the perfectionist, I wasn't satisfied with my marksmanship, but the Colonel was. He told me with a laugh that I shot pretty well for a girl. As we walked back towards the farm house, he asked if I wanted to drop off my bags at my car. I said that I wanted to clean my rifle before putting it away. I could tell that was the right answer immediately, because he kind of slapped me on the back. As we went into the kitchen, he grabbed a large plastic table cloth, and slung it over the dining table. He sat down opposite to me, and seemed to be settling in as if he was going to watch a movie. I realized that I was being tested again.

My father had always taught me that every tool that you use should be put away clean, dry, sharp, and in its place. I have always tried to take care of my tools, and I wanted to look as if I knew everything there was to know about firearm care. I had spent more time picking out the tools to clean and oil my new rifle as I had in picking the weapon itself. I knew from the sergeant first class that had taught my basic firearms class that the nice little cleaning sets that are sold are mostly crap. I had learned to gather my tools separately, and was quite picky about the cleaning solution and oil I used. I took

Curveballs

out the cleaning rod first. I never used aluminum. It gets scratched too easily, so it tends to collect dirt in the creases. I was taught to always use coated nylon rods. When I pulled out this white plastic looking rod, I thought I saw a frown on his face. He said, "You don't use a metal rod?" I told him why I don't use aluminum and that on anything larger than a .22, I'd use stainless steel, but I find that in a .22 bore, that it's such a tight fit, that I risk damaging the rifling in the bore. He got up, and went on to the old sleeping porch. I heard the jangle of keys, and the sound of the large cabinet I had seen in the other room being opened. He came back in the room with half a dozen different sized cleaning rods. He sat them down on the table, and I picked up the closest one, wiped it down with one of my cleaning rags, and showed him that it didn't come clean. You could see that there were a number of small scrapes down the side that remained packed with carbon particles.

    I picked up one of the larger rods that was obviously stainless steel, and wiped it clean as well. This rod was shiny without any residue. I held them up for him to look at closer. All he could say was, "I'll be damned." Then he looked up and met my eyes, and said, "What kind of solvent do you use." I quickly replied, "I only use Hoppes #9," reached in my bag producing a half full bottle, opened it and took a quick smell saying, "I have always loved the smell of the stuff." With that he slammed his hand down on the table, and broke out laughing. He said, "I've never met a woman who knew how to really clean a gun before, and here you are teaching me something new, and I've been shooting since I was old enough to hold one. I also love the smell of Hoppes." I started field stripping and cleaning my rifle almost absentmindedly. I was finally feeling like I could relax a bit. That's scary, and even worse, I was actually starting to like this man.

Chapter 16: In the Rear View Mirror

Once I had my gun cleaned and put away, I decided that I had better make as graceful an exit as I could as quickly as I could. I was getting tired, and I knew that I might slip up if I wasn't completely on my game. He walked me to my car, and opened the door for me. I hadn't locked my car on purpose, but wondered how he knew that. I took a second to look around as I was pretending to fiddle with my keys. Something didn't look right. I thought for a minute that I should just get out of the car, but told myself that I was just being paranoid. I drove across the grounds towards the gate trying not to give council to my fears. I wasn't surprised to see two men at the gate ready to open it for me, and more importantly, lock it behind me. I was so uneasy that when my tires hit the cattle grate on the driveway, it startled me so much; I almost lost control of the steering wheel.

With each mile in the rear view mirror, I felt like I could breathe a little easier. It almost felt as if I had been holding my breath all day long, and my stomach muscles were sore from the effort. Once I made it to the turnpike entrance, I just knew I had to stop and rest for a few minutes. There was a McDonald's just a mile or so inside the turnpike. I pulled into the parking lot, turned off the ignition; put my head on the steering wheel, and just tried to breathe. I don't know how long it took for me to regain my composure, but I finally was able to get out of the car and walk inside. I went to the rest room, and ran cold water on my hands, and put my wet hands on the back of my neck. I wasn't surprised to find the hair standing straight up. I felt like my body was surging with adrenaline.

I walked to the counter, and ordered a very large soft drink. As I walked back to my car, the sun was starting to fade in the sky casting interesting shadows. I noticed there were handprints showing on my hatchback. My car had been cleaned just yesterday. I had filled up for the trip and gotten a free car wash. The dirt on it had come from the dirt road approaching the farm. The handprints must have happened after I arrived at the farm. I took out my keys and carefully opened my back hatch. I almost expected something to jump out at me. Nothing was missing that I could tell, but it was obvious that everything had been touched, moved, or gone through. I didn't keep anything secret or valuable. I had a toolbox with an assortment of tools that I might be called upon to use on my car, a set of jumper cables, a can of WD-40, and some loose camping equipment from my last trip. The strangest thing was probably a small bag of kitty litter that I use in winter for traction, incase I got stuck.

I shut the hatch, and I sat in my seat, and leaned across and opened up the glove box. I kept a plastic folder in there with all my insurance documents and registrations, and the owner's manual. I tried to look at it with the eyes of a stranger. The owner's manual was dog eared on the page for maintenance timetables. I kept detailed records on a small memo book of gas mileage and oil and filter changes. At the very least it made me look anal. I kept gas mileage because it often decreased when something was wrong with the engine. Back when I drove old beat up cars, that was important. I might be driving new cars now, but old habits die hard. There was also a box of Kleenex and cough drops I kept for my bad sinuses. That's the kind of thing my grandmother had in her glove box.

I realized that the most important thing was my stack of registrations and insurance cards. They had obviously been messed with. I was bad about not taking out the old ones when I got new ones, and transferred the whole pile from my old cars into this new one. The old ones had old addresses. I knew without a doubt that they were investigating me, everything about me. I had no idea where this was going to lead me, but one thing was sure, there was no going back now.

The next few weeks seemed like a blur. I tried to go about my every day business. I went to work, I went to church, and I went to my class and meetings just like nothing was different. I was different though. I was going to the farm almost every Saturday. Each week I would see a few more people, doing a few new things. The whole thing seemed orchestrated. I felt like a frog being put into a pot of cold water, and someone was starting to slowly turn up the heat.

Chapter 17: Walking a Tightrope

It was 10 weeks after my first trip to the farm that I saw something that really frightened me. Many of the buildings on the property that we just passed by on our way to other things were securely locked up. When I approached the front gate on this Saturday, I knew things were going to be different. From the road I could see cars and trucks parked all the way to the front fence area. It looked like a used car lot or a swap meet. I thought about driving past, but the men at the gate had already seen me, and were opening the gate for me. There were people milling around everywhere, and they were all carrying guns. I saw two small boys who couldn't have been more than 8 years old carrying shotguns. I wondered where their parents were.

My heart started racing. I could feel sweat beginning to bead on the back of my neck. Every instinct in my body said to run. In a way, I think I was immobilized by the fear, and ended up staying because of it. The man I had met the first week with the German accent came across the grounds to meet me. He said the Colonel had sent him to fetch me because he didn't want me to get lost in the crowd. All the people I saw milling around seemed to be heading towards a small Quonset hut that had always been locked. It looked like the kind of thing that farmers store their lose equipment in. It was far too small to house all the people that seemed to be going inside. I felt like a child at the circus watching a dozen clowns climb into a small toy car. I wanted to stay and watch the procession, but was being lead towards the farm house.

It was surprisingly empty. When I went to the kitchen, the Colonel was sitting calmly at the table having a cup of coffee. He motioned for me to sit down with him. It seemed like an uneasy silence, and I finally said, "I seem to have come to visit at a bad time. Are you having some kind of meeting?" He replied that they had these 3-4 times a year. "I have a lot of friends from all over, and they come to help out on the farm occasionally when I need some extra hands." I told him that it is nice to have friends you can depend on. He seemed to look very serious all of a sudden. He said,

"Yes it is. Now I need to ask you something. Are you a friend? Are you going to be someone I can depend on?" I didn't know what to say. I think I stammered something to the effect that I'd like to think so. He went on to say, "You puzzle me. You grew up in the city, but studied agriculture. We have trouble talking our rural kids into studying that. You're a woman, but can shoot as well as any man I have ever met. You're a Catholic, apparently a devout one by the amount of time you spend at church, but you work with Protestants without trying to convert them. You're obviously bright as a whip, but you have asked me very few questions. People who don't ask questions are either too dumb to, or they already know the answers." He looked at me obviously ready to hear what I had to say.

"I only studied agriculture because they made me. I majored in forestry. That's in the Ag department. If it had been in the Science department, I wouldn't have taken a single agriculture class. I have always loved being in the woods. I don't know why I'm a good shot. My father earned his marksman badge in the Army, so maybe it's genetic. I think I've always been pretty good at things that I like because I put more effort into them. I don't try to convert people because talking about religion always leads to fights, and that touchy-feely kind of stuff makes me uncomfortable. If I don't ask many questions, maybe it's because I don't want to really hear the answers. We are trained in law school to never ask a question in court we don't know the answer to." He looked at me for a moment, and then looked over my shoulder and out the window behind me.

When he looked back at me again, he said, "In the work I do, I'm surrounded by people who just tell me what they think I want to hear. You don't do that. You tell people the truth even when it makes you look bad. The reason I first approached you is a farmer I respect told me that he asked you something, and you admitted that you didn't know the answer, but would try to find out for him, and you did. I've never known any doctors or lawyers or military officers who were ever willing to admit they didn't know something. Brutal honesty and intelligence don't normally go hand in hand. What I need is someone to tell me the truth even when I don't want to hear it."

I looked at him for a moment before replying. "I don't know what you are asking me. I'm not sure exactly what is actually going on here. I get invited to a lot of farms by clients, usually for BBQ's or weddings, and sometimes unfortunately, foreclosure auctions. Yet, I haven't seen any farming going on here. I haven't even seen a piece of farm equipment. I don't know what you want from me." He inhaled sharply, and got up and walked across the room, and poured himself another cup of coffee. When he sat back down, he looked at me and said, "I need some help with some government paperwork. I need someone I can trust, and you have been recommended by every person that I have asked. I'm being sued by the government. I can't find an attorney to represent me in the way that I want to be represented. I want to use my time in court to make the government prove that they have the right to even ask me to be present. I served this country proudly, and it hurts me to see how it has lost its way. Many of my friends have stopped paying taxes. I have surrendered my driver's license. I do not put a tag on my truck. They don't have the right to ask me to. They lost that right when they turned the government over to the Jews.

I want to be a completely sovereign citizen, not a Fourteenth Amendment Citizen. I am subject only to the common law passed down to us by our white ancestors. What I want you to help me with is I want to be completely redeemed from the U.S. Government. You may not realize this, but they enslaved us all by using us as collateral for foreign debt. I need you to help me fill out the forms I need to free myself. I want to be completely free and sovereign from this government so that they no longer have the right to take my farm from me."

I stopped for a moment. In any other place and time, I would have started laughing, but I knew by the cold steel in his eyes, that he was being completely serious. All I could say was, "I've never heard of U.S. citizens being considered as collateral for debt. This is all really new stuff for me, and I'd have to review your paperwork and look this stuff up before I can make any kind of commitment to draw up any paperwork for you. I also would need to check with my Director to make sure that he will allow me to work on it since it is outside my normal duties." He looked at me and said, "That's sounds more than reasonable. Now why don't you come with me. I want to show you off to some of my visitors."

Curveballs

Chapter 18: In the Hornet's Nest

We walked back out the front of the farm house, and made a sharp right hand turn towards the largest of the Quonset huts. There were many children playing in the area around the various huts. All of the adults seemed to be inside. As we went into the building, a man jumped up, and seemed to be coming to attention and saluting us. I realized that he was in fact saluting the Colonel. Everyone seemed to be jumping to attention. There must have been 40 people, mostly men, but some women, scattered around boxes and crates. The room appeared to be some kind of storage facility. What really surprised me is that there seemed to be a lift at the far end that was lowering crates below ground, and I recognized a Halon fire suppression system. I had enough fire training in forestry to recognize it when I saw it. That was a serious, dangerous and expensive piece of hardware for a barn on a farm.

We walked through the crowd to the far side where the lift was located. I had only seen something similar when I was a kid at Carlsbad Caverns. It seemed to be disappearing below ground. I wondered what on earth could be beneath us. From the amount of crates I saw being unloaded off of the back of trucks driven inside, and then lifted below ground, there must have been a very large basement to this Quonset hut. The crates themselves were heavy wooden crates. Each took at least two men to move. Some had black serial numbers written on the outside, but many had been painted over. I wasn't sure what was inside of them, but the smaller boxes were obviously ammunition carriers. I had grown up down the block from a National Guard Armory, and had seen similar boxes unloaded on many occasions. I actually felt bile rising up in my throat.

I wanted to ask to go down below to see what was down there. I wanted to know, but was afraid to at the same time. I finally took a deep breath, and just asked where the boxes were going. The Colonel just waived his hand slightly, and told me that he had dry storage below that kept things more orderly up top. He took his Germanic assistant to one side, whispered something in his ear, and then clapped his hands together sharply. He said after everyone stopped what they were doing, "I'd like to introduce someone that some of you probably already know, or have heard of but never met. This is my new lawyer friend from the Ag Coalition. She's the one your lawyers call when they don't know something. She's been getting to know us, and is trying to decide if she is able to help us put together redemption packets. She's one of the good guys even if she is Catholic." He looked over at me, slapped my shoulder lightly, and said, "We'll have to work on that later." At the last comment, there was a general round of uneasy laughter.

He continued, "She will be getting familiar with our operations over the coming weeks so that she will be better able to meet our legal needs, and we have lots of those my friends." After that there was more laughter and even some light clapping. As he continued talking, I seemed to drift off. I found myself looking around the room at the people. They all looked like the farmers I had been representing all these years, tanned, in worn, but clean clothes. They seemed so normal, except there seemed to be a brightness to their eyes that reminded me of trapped animals. The sound of more laughter brought my attention back. I know he must have said something more about me, because everyone was looking at me. I wished I had been paying attention. I couldn't let my focus fade like that, not now, not here.

When he had finished talking, everyone went back to what they had been doing. The Colonel's assistant had returned from his errand with a clip board that he handed him. He quickly flipped through some papers clipped to it. I wanted to hear what they were discussing, but several farmers that knew me came over to talk to me. I found it bizarre to be making small talk while all around me I got the feeling that I was in the middle of battle preparations. The next truck that came in had crates that were labeled as MRE's. I knew those were the new Army field rations. All I could think of is, "what on earth are they preparing for?"

Chapter 19: Cornered

I kept trying to find a way to leave early. Every time I walked towards the exit, it seemed as if my way was blocked by either a group of people or a large truck. I had never experienced claustrophobia before, but thought that it must feel very much like this. I felt trapped. I actually felt like I was having trouble breathing. I decided to use that excuse. I walked up to the Colonel, and told him that I wasn't feeling well. He could see I was pale and breathless. I lied to him that I had forgotten my allergy medicine that morning, and that something must be flowering on the farm that is setting it off. He started laughing about the forester who is allergic to trees. I laughed and said, "Well, now you know how I ended up in law school."

It was the perfect excuse. Within minutes, I was out of the Quonset hut, and in my car driving down the dirt road and away from the insanity. After 20 minutes, when I was sure that none of the trucks from the farm were following me, I stopped at a large rural convenience store. The smell of broasted chicken filled my nostrils as I entered. I realized how hungry I was. I decided to sit and eat some lunch and try to regain my composure. It seemed such an ordinary thing to sit on one of those molded plastic benches eating chicken. I could feel myself starting to relax.

Just as I was beginning to feel calm again, a strange woman sat down opposite me. She had a similar tray of chicken and potatoes, so at first I thought maybe she was just looking for a place to sit in the crowded seating area. She started to eat without saying anything at first. I had decided to just go about my business, when she finally said, "I don't want to cause a scene in here. I need to know if you are going to cause one. We can do this the hard way or the easy way. The choice is yours." I looked up from my plate, and kind of looked around as if I was trying to decide if she was talking to me or not. I finally replied, "I beg your pardon, were you speaking to me?"

At that she looked at me with cold eyes, and opened her purse to me so that I could see a badge sitting inside. "I have back up outside, I just didn't want to make our presence too visible. We need to have a conversation. You can comply, or we are prepared to take you out of here in cuffs. If you are willing to go peacefully, we will sit here and finish our lunches, then you will hand your keys to me, and I will have someone drive your car to our office while you ride in our car." All I could say was, "what do want with me? I haven't done anything." I got another cold stare from her as she said, "Ms. Reilly, you are an officer of the court. You are required to cooperate with law enforcement. I want to know if you are going to do so." I said, "Of course I am, I just wanted to know what was going on." To that she replied, "We will discuss that later. Why don't you finish your lunch."

    I sat in silence, suddenly no longer hungry. Finally, I realized that it might be some time before I got to eat again, so I forced the rest of my lunch down. I put my keys gently on the table as I got up to throw my trash away. When I returned to the table, my keys were absent. My companion had gotten up, and was walking towards the door. I followed behind her. I noticed my car leaving the parking lot as we neared a non-descript large, dark, sedan. I didn't like the idea that someone else was driving my car. I guess to distract myself from the situation I was finding myself in, all I could think about is that I'd probably have to readjust the seat and mirrors when I got it back. A man was holding the back door of the sedan open for me. I got in, and as he shut the door for me, I had a renewed feeling of being trapped.

Chapter 20: Stupid or Just Crazy

Every question I attempted to ask was met by silence. I finally just rested my head back to watch the scenery go by. Spring time in Oklahoma can be very pretty when there aren't any tornados forecasted. I didn't know what to think. An hour later, I found myself seated in a familiar looking interview room. I had been in many with clients in the past, but this time, the light was pointed my direction. I wondered how long I was going to have to sit in this room before someone came in to explain to me what was going on.

It seemed like I waited a life time. Looking back, it was probably just a few minutes. Two people entered the room finally, a man and a woman, both in dark suits carrying briefcases. The woman sat hers down on the table, and removed a large envelope. Inside were pictures. I realized they were of me, and a cold chill went down my spine. She sat down and pushed them across the table towards me. She said, "Before we start, I would like you to read this card and sign it at the bottom." I picked up the card and realized that I was looking at a Miranda waver card. I felt my fear being replaced by anger. I looked up and said, "I'm certainly willing to sign this because I don't have anything to hide, but before I do, I want to know what is going on here."

The male continued to just stare at me. The woman looked at him, he shrugged, and then she turned to me and said, "We would like to ask you some questions about what you have been doing at Bill Davidson's property. At this point you are not being investigated for anything other than a poor choice of friends." I reached over, signed the Miranda card and replied, "He's not a friend. I've got enough crazy friends without adding him." She picked up the card to make sure I had signed it, and said, "I understand that you are an attorney, but you do have the right to request another attorney be present with you. Are you willing to speak with us without one present?"

I told her again that I hadn't done anything wrong, so she could ask anything she wanted to. The next thing she asked was if I would sign a waver allowing them to search my car. I signed that after

Curveballs

informing her that there was a weapon in the vehicle, but that it was properly secured with a trigger lock and unloaded. She looked at me and told me that they knew there was a weapon in the car, and pulled a picture from the bottom of the stack showing me placing my rifle bag in the hatch. It seemed to have been taken at least a month ago. I asked her why they had been taking pictures of me. The female got up walked across the room, and kind of stared at the mirrored window. She seemed to be trying to decide what to say next.

    She turned back to face me, and said, "We have spent the last couple of weeks turning your life inside out. You make no sense to me. You work non-profit when you could be making 6 figures as a litigator. The attorneys we talked to said you were the nicest person they knew until you entered the courtroom. I understand you even made a judge cry once, yet you spend all your free time either volunteering at church or legal aid or the big homeless shelter. You don't date. You don't have any vices except expensive clothes that we could find. Every person we have asked about you, have said the same thing, that you are just as you seem. So explain to me why you spend half your weekends hanging out with serious scumbags."

    I decided that the truth was the best tact. I explained that I had encountered these guys originally when they started trying to talk my farmers into making foolish financial moves, and I wanted to get more information about them. The more information I got, the worse I felt, and I decided that I wanted to know more, so I just kept trying to get closer to the head guy, and eventually got invited to the farm. The woman, put her hand to her mouth, and laughed out loud saying, "are you telling me that you decided to start your own investigation without any backup?" I said yes, and she said I was lucky to be alive.

    The male investigator spoke up for the first time saying, "We've been trying to get someone onto that farm for over two years, and you're telling us that you talked your way in there in a couple of months?" I shrugged my shoulders and said yeah. Then he started laughing too.

Chapter 21: Setting Boundaries

During the next few weeks, I spent several hours of my free time diagramming for the feds what I had seen and done while on the property. They seemed to know a lot they weren't telling me. They also wanted me to go back and try to get a look at certain specific things. I had already decided that I couldn't in good conscience return to the farm. Once the Colonel had asked me to be his attorney, I couldn't just go spy on him. I refused to discuss anything with them that he had said after asking me to take his case even though I hadn't accepted him as a client. Once someone feels they are covered by attorney/client privilege, I'm not going to violate that. I could tell them anything I saw or heard while other people were around. You aren't deemed to be covered by privilege when other people are involved in the conversations.

The Colonel called me a few days later to invite me out to the farm again. I told him that I couldn't take him on as a private client. I lied to him and blamed my boss and my current work load. He said he was speaking at a rural rally in a couple of weeks, and we could talk more then. I phoned the federal building to talk to the investigators I had been dealing with. They wanted me to go and try to engage him in discussions while other people are present so that I could testify. That was the first time the subject of my testifying in court came up. I didn't think anything about it at the time.

The rally came up pretty quickly it seemed. I was once again in a county park surrounded by pick up trucks and lemonade. This wasn't the same type of presentation that I was used to hearing. This time he was encouraging people to default on their VA guaranteed loans. He said the government would cover the loans for them, that that's what a guaranteed loan meant. I was flabbergasted. He was actually encouraging farmers to get themselves pushed into bankruptcy and foreclosure. I knew that among farmers in Oklahoma, at least half of them probably were veterans and either had VA loans or were eligible to receive them. When he was done speaking, he came

Curveballs

over to me, and asked how the talk went. I just couldn't let it pass. I told him that he was harming these farmers with bad information. He seemed stunned that I would disagree with him. I reminded him that he said he wanted someone to be brutally honest with him. That just seemed to make him madder. I told him that I was going to call every person that I knew at this meeting personally and explain to them how mistaken and dangerous this new idea was. He turned around, and pointed at three men in the crowd, and motioned for them to join him. With three of his posse around him, he seemed quite a bit bigger, and certainly more menacing.

He looked at me with cold eyes, and said, "I was warned not to trust you. You, Catholics are all alike. You are whores of Babylon. You can't be trusted because you have strayed from the true Christian light. You have allowed yourself to be tainted by the mud races. Your race should be your religion. Going against your race is treason, and we know how to deal with that. When the cleansing comes, you and yours will be first." With that he turned and walked away. His cadre stood and stared at me until it was apparent that I was not going to back down and leave. They finally moved away, but followed me for the rest of the afternoon as I walked around to farmers I recognized to talk to them about their VA loans, and advised them not to listen to Davidson.

When I got home that evening, my dog was gone. The gate was left open, and his collar and tags were left hanging on the post. I feared the worst. I started to look for him around the neighborhood. There were a lot of places that he could have wandered off to. Basset Hounds follow their noses, and could be hard to find. I was afraid of what I might find. I decided to walk the route that he often accompanied me when I jogged. Next to a vacant field full of the typical junk you find in the South, rusting car parts, old shopping carts and the like, was my dog. He was fine, and quiet happy to be free of the leash and able to wander where he wanted in the high grass. Going in after him, all I could think about was the possibility of snakes in the grass.

From then on, when I left for the day, I locked my dog inside. He hated it, going so far as to jump through a screen on an open window to get outside. I just couldn't stand the idea that somebody might try to hurt him because of me. When I went out of town on trips, I began leaving him at my mother's house. She didn't seem to mind, and I explained that the neighbors had complained of Buster howling too much when I was gone overnight. Every time I spoke in public on rural issues, I came home to some kind of vandalism. Nothing so serious that it couldn't be explained as the work of neighborhood children, but I just knew he was ordering it.

Chapter 22: Jumping In

About a month before the Colonel's case was to be heard in federal court, I got a call from the US Attorney's office. They wanted me to testify. I was used to being on the other side of the witness box. I knew I needed to talk to my pastor, Fr. Paul about everything. He reminded me of my father in a lot of ways. We had an interestingly strange relationship. I mended his frayed collars and he often played my escort to Bar Association dinners. He actually had a nice suit someone had given him that he wore. I think he liked people to think he was some kind of wealthy guy with a much younger woman on his arm. He loved to dance, and took pleasure in dipping me on waltzes even though he was half a foot shorter than I was. Besides, it was hard for him to pass up $500/plate dinners. I think it gave him something to talk about at his priest support group. I guess he filled in for my deceased father, and I was the daughter he could never have.

To that point I hadn't told any of my friends or family what I had been doing. It was obvious that I was distracted, but that could always be chalked up to having a stressful job. Father Paul could tell something was wrong. He was out walking his dog one evening while Oma and I were trimming the bushes. I guess I was giving the hedges a real beating, and he noticed. We walked by, stopped to evaluate my work, and his only comment was, "Be in my office tomorrow at 2." When I sat down in Fr. Paul's office the next day, he kind of raised his bushy eyebrows waiting for me to start talking. I told him everything. He got up from his chair and walked over to the window and looked outside before responding.

When he turned back around, he asked me if I had pursued these men because of my desire to help my farmers, or for some other personal reason, like excitement or vengeance, or out of some kind of boredom. I told him that I had told myself that what I was doing was out of a sense of trying to do the right thing, but now I wasn't so sure. Maybe it was out of boredom or a desire to feel important. I didn't know anymore about what my motives might have been in the beginning, but the things I had seen and heard while there, firmed my resolve. I might not have had the best intentions in the beginning, but now I was sure of my path. These men were dangerous. They intimidated people who stood up to them.

Fr. Paul sat back down at his desk. He looked at me and said, "You're a good woman. I know that we've talked about how disappointed you were when you felt like you were denied an opportunity to enter a religious order. I think that is where some of this has come from. You aren't the person you thought you were going to get to be, but you haven't really stopped to think about the person you want to be. You've just been flowing with the stream instead of knowing where you wanted to go. Deep down, I think you are still trying to impress your mother and her family with your accomplishments. I also think that taking dangerous chances is your way of trying to show people that you can measure up to your father's bravery. You've spent your whole life trying to measure up to other people's expectations of you."

I didn't know what to say. "You're right. I have let my desired to make my mom happy warp just about everything I have every done. Feeling like I was robbed of my vocation happened over 10 years ago now. I'm no longer a child. I might not have originally picked this path for myself, but I have a good life, and I feel like I'm doing something important. These hate mongers have just made me realize how important. My dad once told me that life is what happens to you while you are making other plans." He looked me straight in the eyes and said, "You need to decide what you want to do with the rest of your life. I think it is time for you to settle down, get married, and start a family before you look up and wonder where your life went."

Wow, he wanted me to get married. I came to talk about whether I should testify, and he wanted me to started having kids. Now that is a proper Catholic priest. I half laughed, and said, "I don't even know how to date, and you want me to run out and start having kids." He said, "I don't want you to run right out and get pregnant, we do frown on that around here. I just think that the path you are going down right now could lead you to be in real danger. Crusaders sometimes don't come home. You are my daughter in the eyes of the Lord, and I am responsible for your well being in a lot of ways. I don't want to see you get hurt. I don't want you to testify."

"I have to testify, Father. Someone has to stand up to them. Last week I had a banker that I had scheduled to come to a mediation hearing ask if our farmer would go through a metal detector before coming to the meeting. He was afraid. Two months ago, we had a farmer's wife call to ask us to warn their county sheriff not to serve the foreclosure notice on her neighbor's place. She said the farm was swarming with men with rifles, and she was afraid for the sheriff's life. We were just able to get a hold of him before he walked into an ambush that I'm convinced this man I'm to testify against had arranged. People are afraid, and they are being taught a warped Christianity as their salvation and as their excuse for doing these terrible things."

Father Paul, replied, "And after you testify, what then?" "Then I'll go back to my job of trying to save as many family farms as I can." He asked back, "Do you want that to be your whole life, your whole world, from now on?" I answered, "No I don't. I'm taking theology classes at night because I eventually want to do some kind of ministry at the Archdiocesan level. I enjoyed the few cases I got to help with in the tribunal. I think though, Social Justice is going to stay my main passion. It always has been. I wanted to enter a religious order not to be a nun, but to be a missionary. I wanted to help people who really needed it. I just ended up finding my mission here." He smiled and said, "I guess you got the answer you were looking for when you came in here then. You are going to testify. You didn't need my advice after all."

The next morning, I called the US Attorney's office, and told them that I would be willing to testify, but I wanted them to subpoena me. I didn't want my farmers to get the wrong idea, and think I was willingly giving information to the government about one of their own. I also knew that my boss would have puppies. We made arrangements for them to serve me at work when I knew everyone would be in the office. It was quite dramatic.

At first everyone looked at me like I was being sued or something. My secretary had been divorced several times (I ended up handling 3 of them over the years), and knew what a subpoena looked like. I called a meeting to explain that the federal government had asked me to testify in a case involving a farmer. This farmer had never been in our office, nor had he ever requested any AG Coalition services. I explained that he had asked me to represent him in a personal matter, and I had declined. I would be testifying to things that were not governed by any apparent attorney/client privilege. They were upset. The hotline counselor was livid. Her world didn't allow for anything that might appear to be a betrayal of a farmer. I explained that this man was one of the ones who were preying on and harming honest farmers. The counselor was un-swayed. My secretary became worried. She knew much more about my dealings with these guys than I realized. She often talked to clients at length before passing them through to me. She knew some of them just wanted to talk, and I didn't have time for that kind of babysitting.

    The next day, I had an appointment downtown to go over my testimony. I had never been in this particular building before. It had two towers, and express elevators. I didn't realize that I had to take a certain elevator in order to end up on the proper floor. I took the wrong one. When I pushed the button for the 10th floor, it wouldn't light up. I assumed that the bulb was burned out. When it went past the 10th floor and stopped on the 12th to let someone else off, I decided to get off too and just walk down the 2 flights of stairs. Big mistake. Once I got in the stairwell, the door locked soundly behind me. I tried to open the door on 10, and it wouldn't budge.

    I was really perplexed. I decided to just walk down to the lobby and start over again. I guess it was about then that I realized I was in the wrong tower. I walked down the additional 10 flights, and found that the first floor door would also not open. I thought I had miscounted, and went down another flight only to find myself in the mechanicals of the building. I was afraid I was going to touch something that would electrocute me.

I decided to walk up each flight, try each door until I found one that opened. The whole thing was surreal. I finally found a door open on the 6th floor. It opened into the back of a law office. A secretary making copies at a Xerox machine looked at me strangely. I just said I got lost on the way to the elevator. She pointed me in the right direction. This time the elevator let me off on the floor I pushed, the lobby.

    I walked across the concourse to a sign listing the offices. It had color codes for the elevator to use. I was at my appointed place, if only a bit late, and covered in sweat from my stair climber exercise. They prepared me with all the questions they were going to ask me, and went over my answers. They weren't attempting to influence my testimony; they just needed to know what I was going to say to each question to gauge how they wanted to present their case. I knew the drill well. What they couldn't prepare me for were the questions the other side might ask.

    It was then that they informed me that Davidson was going to be representing himself in court. He would be asking me any questions he wanted to. They told me he had the option of requesting a deposition from me, but had waived the option. That's when I realized that he knew I was going to testify. I had that familiar sensation of a cold chill going up my spine. Sitting in a sweat filled suit jacket just made it colder.

Chapter 23: Going To Ground

In a way, the closer it got to the trial date, the more afraid I was becoming, but also the more determined. I started getting threatening phone calls. I knew I was being followed because they were coming right up on my bumper. One evening I came home from my night school class to find my bedroom windows shot out, and my dog cowering in fear. My bed was covered in glass. I called the feds, and I was taken out of there immediately and placed in protective custody. My dog was taken to a friend's house to stay. I was placed in a seedy hotel. I've stayed in bunkhouses that smelled better.

They allowed me to go to work, and continue with most of my activities, but I was given a small automatic pistol and a shoulder holster for my protection. They didn't have the manpower to give me a full time body guard, and I refused to just hide in the hotel. I went to class, I went to church, and I went to the office just as always, except at night I returned to the hotel and my matronly roommate. She treated me like I was some kind of mobster informant. I think the funniest thing happened when I decided to ditch my tail one afternoon, and go visit a friend.

Oma was the German bride of a retired Air Force sergeant. She was several years older than I was, but we seemed to have a lot in common. In some ways she was like the older sister I never had. She was a clerk in a western clothing store. During the week, during the day, she had few customers. I often went over in my free time to talk to her and give her some company. I had told her very little about my upcoming testimony. She knew I was going to court, but didn't know why this would be different than any other time I was in court. After my home had been shot at, and I had been removed to the hotel, I was allowed one phone call like the prisoner I was beginning to feel like. I had called Oma. She was worried about me in a way I couldn't allow myself, so I guess I went to see her just so that she could see that I was okay.

We were having our typical visit talking about the grounds keeping at church or something about one of the committees we both served on, or the choir, when I reached for something, and she saw the butt of the pistol under my jacket. She freaked out. I had a good laugh later when she was describing the weapon to her veteran husband. Her hands made it out to have been a foot long cannon. When I told him it was a small .25 caliber automatic, he broke out laughing. There was something about the look in her eyes that made me finally realize this wasn't a game anymore. It seemed like I had to be constantly reminded of that.

The night before my testimony, they let me go home to pick out some clothes to wear to court the next day. I was surprised to see that the plywood I had nailed over my bedroom window had been replaced with a new window. I wondered who had done it. To this day, I just don't know. It might have been the feds trying to make things look natural, but they denied it. It could even have been a neighbor I suppose. I just never found out. I picked out my favorite blue and white striped silk dress, and a blue linen suit jacket to go over it. I seemed to linger over my lingerie drawer a long time. I had never really liked wearing stockings and slips. That day, it just seemed so important. For some reason it reminded me of picking out my father's clothes for his funeral. I guess the difference was that this time, I also had to pick out shoes.

On the way back to the hotel, we passed the Cathedral. It was just time for evening services. I asked to stop. When the mass was over, I still didn't feel like returning to that dreary hotel. I asked the priest if he had time for a quick confession. He looked at me strangely, but motioned me towards the rectory. I told my keepers that I would just be a little longer. They were restless and wanted to order pizza at the hotel. The rector of the Cathedral knew who I was by sight. The Cathedral was the closest church to my office. I often went over for mass on my lunch hour. I also sang with the Archdiocesan Choir, so he had seen me at official functions. He also had called me many times for last minute funeral music.

I had never gone to him for confession before. I usually only went twice a year during the large penitential services we had during Lent and Advent. I found confession to be liberating, but I still hated going. It was kind of like the dentist. Your teeth always feel better after going, but that doesn't make it any easier to get me in the door. He asked if I wanted to go into the confessional, or would I prefer his office. I said his office was more comfortable, and he agreed with me. I couldn't remember ever being in this part of the building before. His office was much larger than Fr. Paul's.

A took a seat across from his desk. He decided to sit in the chair next to me. I said, "Bless me father for I have sinned. It has been 7 months since my last confession." He said, "What's troubling you." I told him I was going to be testifying against the head of a white supremacist group tomorrow. When I told him the name of the group, he dropped the prayer book he was holding. It slammed to the floor and startled us both. He spurted out, "Jesus, Mary and Joseph, I read the New York Times. How on Earth did you get involved with them?!" I told him the story, and how I was starting to get nervous. I guess I was there looking for some spiritual fortitude. He listened to my confession, he prayed with me, and gave me some advice. He said that I should just follow my conscience in my testimony, and not try to either please the government or protect myself from the opposition. He told me to use the truth as my shield, and not to violate anything that might be considered privileged, no matter what.

I left his office feeling much better. I was still afraid, but I was firm in my resolve. That night when I sat down to say my rosary; I took out an old faded, tattered prayer card that my father had carried in his wallet. It was the Memorare prayer written by my father's patron saint. I decided to place it all in Her hands. It took me a long time to fall asleep. I woke up late. My keepers had let me sleep in. I had a time to appear in the afternoon, so I had plenty of time to linger over my shower, and have a long lunch.

Chapter 24: The Other Side of the Bar

I had been in that courthouse many times. I was admitted to the federal bar just a few months after I had been admitted to the state bar. I wasn't used to having to wait out in the hall way. My 2pm time came and went. I didn't even know what was going on in the court room. When they took a break, I went outside and grabbed one of the last hotdogs off of a vendor's cart, and decided to use a pay phone. While I was on the phone, a bailiff came outside freaking out that I had taken off without telling them. I gave him a raised eyebrow, and went back to my phone call. I had called Oma. They were expecting me at church that night, and I didn't want her to worry that something had happened to me.

When I finished my call in my own time, I allowed the bailiff to escort me back inside the building. I finally heard my name called at 5:30pm. I had actually zoned out a bit, and didn't hear them the first time. As I walked up the aisle almost everyone was turning to stare at me. Davidson didn't turn around until I was almost to the front. He seemed surprised to see me there. I almost tripped climbing up into the witness box. I never noticed before that there was a step there, and I was distracted by the judge. He was one of my old law school professors. I knew he had been named to the bench, but I didn't expect to see him sitting there. The court clerk handed me a bible, and I swore to tell the truth. I remember once having a law school professor tell me that saying the oath is meant as a way to remind the witness how serious the situation was. He was right.

The prosecutor went through a list of my credentials since they were going to use me as both an expert witness on farm finances and as an eyewitness to the actions of the defendant. That's very unusual, and there would normally be a taint of bias on the part of an expert witness also testifying as an eyewitness. The problem is that there were very few attorneys at that time who could have testified as an expert witness on the issues that family farmers were facing in Oklahoma.

I could see the Colonel sitting across the room at his table. He was alternately glaring at me, and writing on a legal pad in front of him. After my credentials were presented, he asked for a side bar conference. I couldn't really hear what they were discussing. I didn't want to look around the room. So I just looked down at my feet while they were talking. My most vivid memory is sitting there and smelling Murphy's Oil Soap. Someone must have polished up the wood railing and bench with it. I had been in enough trouble growing up at school that I had many opportunities to use Murphy's as penance on the church pews.

When their conference was over, the US Attorney requested that the court accept me as an expert witness, and the Colonel didn't object. They asked me a variety of questions about my experiences in trying to restructure farm loans, deal with the tax implications of a large restructure plan, and other viable options for distressed family farms. After that they asked my experiences in dealing with farmers who had used sight drafts and other types of bogus commercial paper to try to save their farms. I recounted the nightmare of trying to sort it all out, and that I had been unable to save a single farm that had gone down that path.

As I said the last part, I looked straight at Davidson. He was writing furiously. He looked up, and I met his gaze. I wasn't afraid. I wasn't going to remain silent. As we had discussed in our preparations, she asked me no questions about the activities I saw at his farm. Those things would wait until the major criminal case. This case dealt exclusively with the financial aspects of his dealings with the government, and his trying to encourage others to engage in similar fraudulent activities. I answered all her questions as clearly and concisely as possible without elaborating. I had enough experience with cross-examination to know what a pitfall that can be.

When she had rested her direct examination, the Colonel cleared his throat and stood up. He began to walk towards the witness box. The US Attorney jumped to her feet and objected. The judge explained to him that he would have to ask his questions from the lectern, and could not approach the witness without permission. He looked at me and said, "Certainly your honor. I wouldn't want to intimidate the witness in any way." Since I had said that none of the farmers who had used his sight drafts had been able to save their farms, he started there. He questioned how many farms I had been able to save through mediation and restructuring. I told him that to that point I had participated in over 300 mediations, and we had saved every one of those farms except for one, and that farmer didn't want to farm anymore.

He looked like he wanted to contest my answer, but then saw me reaching for my satchel. He knew I had come prepared and didn't want me to be able to speak about it any further. He then started in on his new VA guaranteed loan scheme. I made it clear that he was at best mistaken, and at worst he was doing real harm to farmers. He lost his temper. He started raising his voice and moving past the lectern. He started to question my credentials. The judge reminded him that my credentials had already been accepted. He proceeded to ask me questions in a rapid fire manner trying to trip me up. He didn't succeed.

Finally he seemed to be at the end of his patience. He continued to raise his voice. The judge admonished him several times. He grilled me for over an hour. I didn't waver. He didn't trip me up, and at the end we both were exhausted. He finally rested his cross-examination. The US Attorney had no further questions either. She looked exhausted just from watching us spar. I was excused, and the judge adjourned the court for the day. As I walked outside the courtroom, my keepers had reappeared. They said they were going to escort me down the back way for my protection.

I ended up riding down the private elevator with the judge. He mentioned that he noticed I had attended OU. I said yes, and I had been in his class. He asked which one. I listed off the 3 classes I had with him. He was very upset that he didn't remember me. I explained that I had lost weight, and he had probably never seen me in something other that sweat pants or blue jeans. We of course didn't discuss the case, but as I was exiting the elevator on the parking level, he told me to be careful. The agents took me back to the hotel. I walked inside, packed my things, put them in my car, and drove away over their vehement objections. I wasn't going to spend one more minute hiding. I was convinced that all their threats and harassments would end because they were designed to prevent me from testifying, and that was over now.

I didn't even drive home. I knew that it was adult education night at church. That was practically our social evening and people would expect to see me there. I drove straight over. I needed to see my friends. When I came inside the parish hall, it was the break time, and I saw many relieved faces, and got lots of enthusiastic hugs. Everyone was so happy to see me. It really made me realize how important that parish was to me. I stayed around for a little while afterwards helping clean up. Father Paul caught me outside in the hallway. He wanted to know if it was really over. I told him I thought it was. He said he wanted me to take tomorrow off, sleep in, and in the afternoon, he wanted me in his office at 1pm. All I could say was, "Yes sir."

Chapter 25: Dolly Levi

I went directly from church to my friend's house to pick up my dog. He was so excited to see me, he practically jumped up into my arms, and for a Basset Hound, that's saying something. I ended up covered in drool. I went home, and dropped my bags just inside the front door. I was so happy to be home, that I didn't even look around. I just fell into bed with Buster at my side. When I finally opened my eyes the next day, the sun was starting to get high in the sky. I could hear Buster outside running the back fence with the neighbor's dog. I'm glad I had remembered to unlock his dog door before going to bed. He must have heard me moving around because he came inside, grabbed his empty dog bowl, and slammed it to the kitchen floor to get my attention.

After feeding him, I took a long soak in the tub. I threw on some jeans, and headed over to church. Fr. Paul was around on the side of the rectory that faced the cemetery next door. He once joked that his neighbors were very quiet, and that when he passed, we could just throw him over the fence. He was walking his dog, and waved at me. I went in the rectory front door, and gossiped with the church secretary while I was waiting on Fr. Paul to come in. I heard him come in the back door. His dog appeared first. He had to come in and get his hugs.

Fr. Paul made his appearance in due time. He never hurried. He walked over to his office door, turned around and crooked his finger at me. I was officially summoned. He sat down behind his desk, and looked at me for a moment. He said, "You know you're not the easiest parishioner I ever had. You had us all pretty scared, and I want you to promise you won't get into any more messes like this. I've got enough gray hair as it is." All I could do was apologize for worrying everyone. He went on by saying that he wanted to continue the conversation we had started several weeks ago.

"I want you to seriously think about settling down. If you want to have children, it isn't a good idea to wait until you are over 30. When was the last time you went on a date?" I had to admit to him that I hadn't been on a real date in well over 12 years. I couldn't pretend with him. I couldn't lie to him like I did so often with my friends. It was excruciating to have to admit. I started crying. He came around the desk, and sat next to me. He put his arm around my shoulder, and said, "You faced down neo-Nazis without a tear, and now start crying because you haven't had a date in 12 years." I said, "I'm not crying because I haven't had a date. I'm crying because it is so hard to admit. Everyone around me has more experience than I do. Most 14 year old girls have more experience than I do, and it's embarrassing."

He started rubbing my shoulder until I stopped crying. He got up and retrieved his box of tissues. I got the distinct impression that his box was well used. I felt relieved and humiliated at the same time. I really hated showing any vulnerability. He went back behind his desk. I think he knew that I needed some space. When I had finished blowing my nose, he asked very quietly, "Catherine, are you trying to tell me that you've never been with a man?" I whispered yes. He said, "Why are you embarrassed by that. I've had women sitting in that same chair crying about their pasts of too many men, or horrible diseases that have left them infertile. You don't have anything to be ashamed of, far from it."

I looked at him and said, "My mom wants to know when I'm going to get married. All my college friends are married, most with children already. I don't know how to do this stuff. I really had always planned to be a nun, and I just pushed that part of my life into the background. I think it is too late to start now." He replied, "That's ridiculous. You just need to get over your fear, and try to meet the right man." I responded that I wouldn't know what to do. I didn't know the first thing about how to meet a man, where to do it, or even how to act on a date. He looked at me and said, "Didn't your mother ever talk to you about this kind of stuff." I told him no. I told him that when it came to relations or relationships, I had been taught nothing. I had had sex education in school, but other than the plain biological aspects, I had no knowledge whatsoever.

He started writing something down in a notebook. He said he was writing a list of chores he wanted me to do. He wanted me to read a book he was

Curveballs

handing me, he wanted me to go on a simple date with a safe person within the month, and he would arrange it. He had a list of 5 women from the parish that he knew I was friends with. He wanted me to have at least one discussion with each of them about how they had met their husbands. He told me that he was going to meet with me once a month until he was satisfied that I was making an effort. He said, "I don't want you to be sitting in that chair 20 years from now lamenting your missed opportunities. Now I want you to go do something fun for the rest of the afternoon. No work, no schoolwork, no housework. Go to the movies, the mall, somewhere you don't normally go, and look around. You never know, you might fall in love at first sight."

Chapter 26: Everything is Peachy

The next couple of months seemed to move at a blistering pace. Even though I felt safe, I thought it was best to take some precautions. I continued to carry a weapon for almost 6 weeks until it started to chafe me. I varied my routine of where I went to lunch, the direction I drove to work and church, and I started locking my fence and property more diligently. There were a few times I felt like I might have been followed, but there was no re-occurrence of the intimidation tactics I had been subjected to prior to my testimony. I started to relax.

As ordered, I went on a date with someone to the movies. He was someone from church who was a bit older than I was, and disabled from a bad car accident. Kevin was already a friend, so that made it easier. If getting fixed up on a date by my pastor seemed strange, it didn't occur to me because the idea of dating in general seemed strange. We went to a horrible Sylvester Stallone movie. I don't even remember the name of it now. I also did the driving, so I didn't have the discomfort of wondering if he was going to want me to invite him inside my home. When we got to his house, he invited me inside for some tea. I was afraid to go inside with him, so I excused myself.

This went on for several weeks. Every Friday night we would go to the movies. On Saturdays, I played guitar routinely for the vigil mass. He started to come and sit in the pew next to the choir area. People began to notice. One of my friends from church asked me if we were getting serious. I didn't know how to respond. When Fr. Paul hauled me into his office a few weeks later, I thought it was to ask how things were going. Instead he looked upset. He told me that he thought I should stop seeing Kevin. That it had been a mistake for him to arrange for us to date. I was stricken. I thought that he had heard we had been doing something we shouldn't have.

He looked at me and said, "I'm sorry, but I can't really discuss this with you. It would violate his privacy. One of the first rules about dating that I try to instill in the youth group here is that you should never date someone you can't marry. You've had canon law and worked at the tribunal, so you should understand that. I can't really say anything else." After that Kevin started attending masses he knew I wouldn't be at. Being in the music department, our schedules were arranged well in advance, so it was easy for him to find out when I was singing.

The next person Fr. Paul fixed me up with was a new parishioner. He was from Texas and worked at the Air Force Base near by as a civilian contractor. After a couple of months of regular dates to movies and dinner, I took him to Thanksgiving dinner at my mother's house. It was the first time that anyone in my family had ever seen me with a boyfriend. They were stunned and didn't know what to make of it. He was quite a bit shorter than I am, but was Hispanic and reminded me of my Godfather a bit. He wanted me to come house shopping with him. I thought that meant he was serious. Fr. Paul cracked quite a large smile when I told him. He said that was a positive sign that José was also ready to settle down, and that if he wanted me to see the houses, that meant he probably was serious about our relationship.

Fr. Paul got serious then, and wanted to know if we were spending any time alone together. He told me he wanted me to be careful to not place myself in a position where José might get the idea that I was ready for intimacy. I told him that we hadn't done anything beyond very quick good night kisses. Fr. Paul seemed relieved and puzzled at the same time. José went home to Texas for Christmas. He called me when he got back, and told me he had something big to tell me. I was terrified he was going to ask me to marry him. Instead, he informed me that he had gotten engaged to his former childhood sweetheart back home. I was crushed and relieved at the same time. Fr. Paul was livid. He thought that José had used me to manipulate his fiancé into accepting his proposal. José started attending another parish, and I decided it was time I found my own boyfriends.

Right after Christmas that year, I was visiting an older woman from church. She didn't drive, and I would often drive her and her sister to the mall to do some shopping. She had a border living with her that kind of took care of things around her house as part of his rent.

That afternoon, he had a friend visiting. They were sitting in the living room watching TV as Jane and I came in from shopping. He stared at me in a way that I was not used to men staring at me, or maybe had just not noticed before. I thought giving him one of my glares would get the message across. He didn't notice my glare because he wasn't looking at my eyes. I was extremely perturbed. I finally crossed my arms across my chest, and said very firmly, "Excuse me; I don't appreciate what you are doing. I'm not a piece of meat to be stared at."

He acted as if he didn't hear me. I waved my hand at him to get his attention, and said, "Didn't you hear me. Stop staring at me." Jane's border elbowed his friend, and said, "Don't waste your time on the Ice Princess. She won't give you the time of day." I was offended and said, "I don't know what you are talking about," and stormed into the kitchen to sit with my friend. We were having a cup of tea later when his friend came into the kitchen. He said, "I'm sorry if I offended you, I've just never seen anyone so pretty before." I was dumbstruck. No one had ever said anything like that to me before. He was tall and slim and had a short beard. His name was Ken, and it was the start of the first real relationship I had ever had.

Chapter 27: The World is Spinning

We started dating almost immediately. He wasn't Catholic, but I told myself that was easily remedied. He worked at his brother's business making wooden shutters. He often worked late shifts, and didn't get off until 11pm at night. That made going out to movies kind of difficult, but left me plenty of time to continue with my private clients. We still spent a lot of time together. At first, we only met at Jane's house. He lived with his parents, so her house seemed the perfect place to get to know each other. He took me to meet his brother and sister-in-law. They really seemed to like me, and we had a great time. That night after having dinner at his brother's house, I drove him home. Before he got out of my car, he leaned across and gave me the longest kiss I had ever had. My knees went weak, and my whole body started to tingle. It was almost an overwhelming feeling for me.

I went home and had trouble sleeping. I was confused and scared, and I didn't understand why I was feeling that way. The next day he called me at work. He said his mother had teased him because he had my makeup on the collar of his shirt. He wanted to know if he could take me out to dinner that night. I decided to take the plunge and invited him to my house for dinner. I left work early, and was so nervous that I must have made enough food for 10 people. He just laughed when he saw the table covered with dishes. After dinner we watched a movie sitting on my couch together. He put his arm around me, and we eventually started kissing again. He gently started to lean me back on the couch, and I began to get uncomfortable and panicky. I turned my head away, and said, "No Ken, we can't be doing this."

Instead of stopping, he began to kiss my neck since my head was turned. He ran his hand behind my thigh, and tried to lift my leg up onto the couch. Now I was scared. I told him no more forcefully. I said this wasn't proper, and he needed to stop. When he didn't, I used all my strength to push him off me. He was really angry, and shouted, "What's your problem? If you didn't want to do it, you shouldn't have invited me over. What are you, a tease?" I started crying. He looked at me really funny, and came over and sat down next to me. He handed me a tissue from the end table. I wiped my eyes. He apologized for calling me a tease, and then asked why I was crying. I told him that I was a Catholic, and we aren't supposed to let things get out of hand before we marry.

   He started laughing. He said, "You're kidding right?" I told him I wasn't kidding, it wasn't a joke, and my faith was important to me. He got angry again and said, "So you're telling me that you won't sleep with me unless we get married. That's nuts. Didn't all your other boyfriends have a problem with that?" I told him that I'd never been serious enough with a boyfriend before to discuss it. He had a shocked look on his face, and said, "Are you trying to get me to believe that you're a virgin? Aren't you kind of old?" I started crying again. He put his arms around me, and said, "God, I'm sorry. I just never had a girl who was a virgin before. That's actually kind of exciting."

   He tried pushing me back on the couch again. He caught me off guard, and got on top of me. He had my arms trapped against his chest. When he tried to push his knee in between mine, I used all my strength and the experience of wrestling with my older brothers to roll us off the couch onto the floor. I scrambled to my feet, and picked up the softball bat that I kept behind the front door. I shouted at him, "How dare you! Get out, and don't come back, or I'll use this on you." He stormed out screaming for me not to call him ever again. I was shaking in anger, not fear. I had really wanted to hit him with my bat.

   I got in my car and drove over to church. I found Oma out front pruning the rose bushes. She could tell I was upset and asked me what was wrong. I said, "Ken and I just broke up." She asked what had happened, and I told her that he had tried to force himself on me. She asked very concerned if he had hurt me. I told her the only thing he had really hurt was my feelings. I said, "I don't care what Fr. Paul says, I'm just not cut out for this stuff." She said that I shouldn't give up, that the right person would come along eventually, that the trick was to not pass them by when they do.

I just threw myself back into my work. I worked early, late, even weekends. I ran the stairs at the pastoral center during the break in my classes. It was as if I was running away from something full speed. Several months later, right after Easter, I ran into Ken again accidentally at Jane's house. We didn't speak. He rushed past me and got in his truck to leave. Late that night, I was woken up by the sound of the phone. Calls in the middle of the night always get my heart racing. When I picked it up, all I heard at first was silence.

Eventually, I heard a voice say, "I'm sorry. I never got a chance to tell you that." I realized it was Ken talking to me on the other end. I asked him what he wanted. He said he didn't want anything except to hear my voice. Finally, he said, "I'd like another chance, if you're not seeing someone else." I told him that we would have to have some firm ground rules. He agreed to every one of them. He seemed truly contrite. So I decided to give him a second chance. My friends all thought I was making a mistake.

Chapter 28: Mr. Hyde

Ken and I dated for the next 6 months. I tried getting him to come to church with me, but he didn't want to. That seemed to concern Fr. Paul more than it did me. I had grown up in a house with a Catholic married to a Protestant. My mother had taken instruction, and I just felt like it was a matter of time before Ken came around. Besides, I told myself that women are just more religious than men anyway. Our favorite pastime was spending Saturdays at the public swimming pool. I loved the water. The Midwest City pool had a really great diving board. One afternoon, after I had made a dive and swam to the ladder on the side, a man put his hand down to help me out of the pool. As I took his hand, he commented that I had made a great dive.

By this time, Ken had reached the ladder as well. When he got out of the water, he shoved the other man back away from me telling him, "Keep your hands away from my girlfriend." The other man beat a hasty retreat, and I just stood there not knowing what to make of it. I explained that he had only complimented me on my dive. Ken said, "I saw him looking down your suit when he was helping you out of the water. You're too stupid to have noticed I guess." I just told him that he was over-reacting, and if he was going to act that way, I was going to go home.

That seemed to calm him down and he apologized. We sat in a familiar spot under the shade of a tree right outside the fence surrounding the pool. I was just lying back enjoying the warmth of the day, and all of a sudden he threw his towel over my legs. I opened my eyes and looked over at him. He said, "People can see your stuff in that suit." I said, "No one is looking at me, and I'm hardly wearing a bikini you know." He got angry, and said we were leaving. Since we had come in his truck, I didn't want to get stranded there, so I went with him. It just seemed so odd that all of a sudden he seemed to be jealous. It made me self conscious, and I started to look around to see if anyone was actually looking at me. I did see one man. He was outside the fence sitting on a picnic table. He looked very familiar.

I'm not sure what unnerved me more, Ken's new jealousy, or the feeling again that I was being watched. I had relaxed over the last several months, and had fallen back into a familiar routine. I had my yearly physical exam that week. My doctor was actually a good friend. She taught at the medical school. Every time I went to see her we had this friendly banter about whether she needed to bother running a pregnancy test on me before doing any X-rays. I always said no, and that she would be the first to know if I did. This year, I said, no, but maybe this time next year. She was stunned.

"Does that mean what I think it does? Do we need to have a discussion about birth control finally?" I told her no, that wasn't necessary, and was never going to be necessary. She chuckled, and said, "Catholics. So what is his name, and what does he do; how long have you been seeing him?" I told her 6 months. She looked at me again and asked if I sure I didn't want to have a discussion about birth control, and started to dig out a package of condoms to hand me. I waved my hand at her and said, "No, really, that isn't necessary." She put them away, and said, "Okay, but if you do plan on becoming sexually active, I want you to have him tested first and use a condom. I don't have to tell you that there are some nasty things running around out there."

She wanted to know if I had been having any specific problems, and I told her my stomach had been bothering me again. She wanted to know if I had been using any aspirin. I reminded her I couldn't take aspirin. I had fractured my nose and right cheek when I was 14. A softball to the face will do that. It had caused perennial sinus problems including nose bleeds. In college, after having surgery, I had been given some aspirin that started a nose bleed that wouldn't stop and put me in the hospital for 3 days. I had always bruised easily and had problems with clotting, so aspirin is a no-no.

She asked me to describe the way my stomach was feeling, and I said it was like the butterflies I used to get before big games or tests. My mom used to call it a nervous stomach. My doctor thought that I might be developing an ulcer, or it might just be love sickness, but to come back if it got any more uncomfortable. She told me to try eating soft, bland food for a few days to see if it went away.

Other than that, I got my usual clean bill of health. The biggest non-orthopedic problem I had was low cholesterol. I struggled to keep it above 75, when the rest of the country seemed to be trying to lower theirs. My doctor had researched it many times, and she couldn't find any reason for my cholesterol to be so low except that it might just be genetic. This time, she said my blood pressure seemed a bit elevated, and wanted to know when I had last taken a vacation. I couldn't remember. She actually got out her prescription pad and wrote on it "One Vacation, take as needed." I told her I'd see her next year, and she replied, "Or before then if there's any changes."

Chapter 29: Mexico

As I left the doctor's office, I was overwhelmed with the feeling that I was being watched. I was in the lobby of the large medical complex where her offices are, and was surrounded by people, but still, something was bothering me. I decided I was just being silly, but still, I went a different direction back to the office. I decided maybe she was right, I needed a vacation. When I got back to the office, I looked over my calendar and decided to block off some time in July. I just had to decide where I wanted to go. The first thing that came to mind was this little hotel on the Mexican coast in Puerto Vallarta. It had an open air bakery on a terrace overlooking the ocean. I used to love sitting there, smelling the fresh bread, and reading a book. I was convinced, and called my travel agent to set it up.

That night at dinner, I told Ken I was going to take a trip. He asked if he could come too. I didn't know what to think about that. I decided that perhaps his recent jealousy was the product of his needing a vacation as well, so we talked about the ground rules. We could get adjoining suites, but would have separate bedrooms. He held up his hand and swore that he would respect my space. I still wasn't sure it was a good idea, but I was actually kind of excited at the prospect of showing him the Mexico I loved.

If Ken was excited at going away with me, Father Paul was decidedly upset. We had a discussion about appearances and public scandal, etc. I teased him that he was just trying to figure out a way to get invited along as a chaperone. He asked if I had been spending any time alone with Ken in private. I said he had been at my home many evenings, but had been completely behaving himself. I told him that he was being an old curmudgeon and worrying himself for no good reason.

When I went down the next week to pick up the tickets, I discovered that Ken had called and changed the hotel reservations for us. He had moved us from the little Mexican owned hotel I loved to the Holiday Inn. At first I was furious thinking that he had tried to move us into a one bed suite. My agent was apologetic saying that she thought he was calling on my behalf. She assured me that we would still have separate bedrooms. He had apparently been afraid of staying someplace unfamiliar, and the Holiday Inn sounded safer to him. I was exasperated, but decided to make the concession if it made him more comfortable. The Holiday Inn was in the North Hotel zone, a new area at the time. I preferred being on the South side of Banderas Bay, but decided not to make a big fuss. The Holiday Inn did appear to have a very nice pool area, so I acquiesced.

    The day of departure arrived, and Ken seemed as excited as a kid on Christmas Eve. I was going to rest, but it seemed like he wanted to do one of everything. By the time we got to the hotel, it was late in the day, so I took him for a walk on the malecon. It was a boardwalk along the bay downtown, and I thought it would be a nice first night to watch the sun go down over the bay. I did notice that Ken seemed uncomfortable. He made me do all the arrangements when we checked in, and I could swear that he wouldn't actually look anyone in the eyes. I chalked it up to him being tired.

    We walked hand in hand along the malecon, and watched the sun go down by the dolphin statues. I pointed up towards the golden crown topping Our Lady of Guadalupe. It is such a beautiful church. I told him about seeing it for the first time as a child, and thinking what a pretty place it would be to have a wedding. Ken didn't say anything. He was too busy taking in all the sights. On the way back to the hotel, he had the taxi driver pull over. We got out, and he said he was hungry. He took me into the Pizza Hut. I was already going to endure the Holiday Inn, so I knew I was going to have to have a talk with him about coming to Mexico to embrace the culture, not avoid it.

    When the waiter came over to take our order, he spoke to us in English. Most people who work in the service industry in Mexican tourist areas speak English. He even handed us English menus. He probably assumed if we spoke Spanish that we wouldn't be at the Pizza Hut. Ken took the menu, read it, and then pointed to something on it. He then shrugged his shoulder at the waiter while looking at me. He seemed to want me to do all the talking. So I did, in Spanish. I complimented the waiter on his English and told him what we wanted to eat. He smiled at me, took the menus back, and said in Spanish that he hoped we would enjoy our meals.

When the waiter had gotten out of ear shot, Ken grabbed my wrist and asked what I had said to the waiter. He seemed really angry. I explained that I had just complimented him on his English, and apologized for doing it. Normally I would never have had a conversation in a foreign language in front of someone who didn't speak it. I've always thought it was rude, but I guess I was trying to make the point to Ken that we weren't in the US anymore. He seemed to calm down, but every time our waiter came into the dining area, Ken kept a very close eye on him.

We returned to the hotel after eating, and went back upstairs. At home I had always slept in t-shirts, but decided to buy some pajamas for the trip so that I could feel comfortable sharing a sitting room with Ken. I changed into them and my robe. I still felt very self conscious. I was grateful that Ken seemed very tired, and immediately retired to his room. I stood on the balcony feeling the cool night air bring in some soft rain. The smell of the tropical flowers outside the window was intoxicating. My doctor was right. I had needed a vacation.

I always seemed to wake up very early when on vacation. I took a walk down by the water to watch the men fixing their fishing nets. This was the part of Mexico that tourists rarely take the time to see. As I was walking back, I decided to surprise Ken with one of my favorite things to do in Mexico. I went upstairs to find him awake and upset that I had left without him. When I told him I was arranging a surprise for him, he calmed down and got excited. I took him down to the beach, and showed him the horses I had hired for the morning. His eyes got as big as saucers. He had never been on a horse before which for an Okie was strange. We road the horses along the bay for about 30 minutes, and stopped at a little grotto area. I helped him off, tied the horses up, and unpacked the picnic breakfast I had arranged for on my way upstairs.

The local yogurt was thick and the granola crunchy. I took out a large mango, and told him that we had to eat it in the water because they were so juicy. I waded out into the water about waist deep. Ken seemed hesitant at first, but finally went in after me. I sliced the mango, and fed him a piece. He had never been in the ocean before. He'd never eaten a mango before. I'm not sure that he had ever been out of Oklahoma before. I ran back through the water, and grabbed my bag. I had stowed one of my favorite kites inside. Flying kites is something I have always loved. I could just afford more expensive ones now than I had as a kid. We took turns flying my parafoil over the ocean for the rest of the morning. I had some trouble getting him back on his horse, but we returned them in one piece, each full of left over granola.

    I again noticed that Ken wouldn't look at the horse owner. He seemed to be unwilling to engage any of the locals. After several days of doing nothing but sitting around the pool relaxing, I drug him downtown to do some shopping at the Mercado. I always wanted to scrounge around for beads to use for making rosaries, and my mother had put in a request for a large bottle of Mexican vanilla. I picked out some onyx beads that were shaped like pyramids. I thought they would make a great rosary for my Godmother for her birthday next month. He bought a few touristy souvenirs for his family. I told him I was going to buy souvenirs at the grocery store. He thought I was nuts, so I made him go with me. The grocery store was a large, modern facility, but it carried things we couldn't get at home. I hit the spice aisle. My Godmother had also sent me with a list of things to bring home.

    Ken stopped in the deli area where many large servers were filled with pre-made entrees. When I walked up to him, he said, "I've never seen anything like this stuff." I pointed out the tongue and tripe. He looked shocked that Mexicans ate that kind of thing. I told him that we were going to go out tonight to a restaurant I knew about run by a distant relative of my Godmother's. I would make sure he had an authentic taste of Mexico while we were here. He had insisted we do most of our eating in the restaurants at the hotel. I had to do all the ordering and paying because he just wouldn't speak to any of the locals. What I thought at first was just

Curveballs

discomfort, was starting to look like something very different.

Chapter 30: Soaring and Crashing

I put on a nice suit for dinner, and we caught a cab downtown. I had to have a long conversation with the driver about where I wanted to go since it was off the beaten track. I noticed Ken's grip on my hand had gotten uncomfortably tight. We arrived at the restaurant. The man at the door looked at us funny. This restaurant was always filled with locals, not tourists. I asked to see Trina. When she came out of the kitchen, she looked at me for a minute, but when I reminded her of who I was, I got a big hug. She then hugged Ken, and he looked like he was going to pass out. We got the royal treatment. She introduced me all around, and asked me what I had been eating that I had gotten so tall.

We had a great meal with liberal amounts of pulque thrown in. That's a kind of home made Mexican beer with the consistency of mucus. It's made by fermenting the leftovers from making tequila. Ours had been heavily laced with sweet pineapple juice, so we drank more than we should have. The meal was a symphony of home made tortillas filled with a variety of different fillings. I decided not to tell Ken about the iguana. I told him it was chicken. Dessert was more alcohol with sopapillas.

As we were walking from the restaurant back towards the malecon, I realized I was intoxicated. My whole body was practically numb. We ended up on a bench down by the dolphin statues, just watching the waves crash on shore. All of a sudden, Ken grabbed my hand, and said, "Catherine, I think we should get married." I was stunned. All I could say was, "Are you sure? Okay." I don't know if it was the alcohol or not, but I didn't know what else to say.

We caught a cab back to the hotel, and I once again sat on the patio watching the water. It was our last night in Mexico, and I just wanted to breathe in every moment. This time instead of watching Mexican cable, he came out and sat with me. We sat in silence for a time, and then I said that we should come back here every year on our anniversary. He didn't say anything to that. After a time, I gave him a good night kiss, and excused myself to retire. I had just been in my room for a few minutes, long enough to take off my watch and glasses when Ken knocked on the door. He asked if he could speak to me for a minute. I put my robe back on, and opened the door.

He put his arms around me saying that he just wanted to hold me for a minute. He began to kiss me much more passionately than I would normally have allowed, and I realized that I was still intoxicated. My body began to feel strange, and I could feel myself relaxing in his arms. He undid the belt on my robe and placed his hands on my back. The shear material of my silk pajamas allowed me to feel the warmth of his hands. He started to breath heavily. I began to feel very uncomfortable, and pulled away. I said, "We can't do this. I won't. You need to leave."

His response was, "Not this time. I've waited long enough, and now that we are getting married, you're gonna give me what I need." With that he pushed me back onto the bed. I found it hard to struggle. His weight was on top of me, and my arms had become entangled in my robe. He started kissing my neck and throat. I continued to tell him no. Finally he rocked up on his knees that he had straddling my waist, and attempted to open my blouse. I was able to free my hands, but he still tore two of the buttons loose. With that I became so angry that I hit him with my right closed fist as hard as I could across the face. He flew off the bed onto the floor. He ended up sitting on the floor at the foot of the bed holding his jaw. I stood up clutching shut my torn top, and screamed at him to get out or I would really hurt him. He quickly skidded across the floor and not only left my room, he left the suite with a slam of the door. I locked him out.

I was so full of anger and adrenaline, that I paced the floor for several minutes muttering to myself like I was preparing a court summation. I just didn't understand how someone could ask me to marry him, and then treat me so roughly. I fell asleep that night sitting out on the balcony. I awoke to the sounds of birds singing, and the smell of an ocean breeze. Shortly afterwards, I heard a knock at the door. I tightened my robe closely around my body, and cracked the door with the chain still attached. All I could see was a large bouquet of flowers. I reluctantly let him in.

He apologized for his behavior, and blamed it on the alcohol. I accepted his apology, but told him that I wouldn't tolerate any more of his aggressive advances. I also apologized for hitting him. I told him that kind of violence had no place in a marriage, and I would never do that again. He had a puzzled look on his face, and then said, "Marriage? Oh that, I was just kidding about getting married." I looked at him in stunned disbelief. I wondered how someone could joke about something that serious. He went over and turned the TV on. I went into my room, and packed my luggage except for my bathing suit and the clothes I was going to wear home on the plane. I put my swimsuit on, and went out and told him that I was going for one last swim.

When I went downstairs, the boys were still cleaning the pool, so I sat on one of the chaise lounges reading my book. When they were done, I slipped into the water and began doing lazy laps. After about 30 minutes, Ken joined me fresh from a shower wearing clean clothes. He said he wanted me to go to breakfast with him in the hotel. I told him I wasn't hungry. He said I needed to come with him now. He said it loud enough that some of the attendants began to look our way. I realized that I didn't really want to make a scene, so I quietly got out of the water, went upstairs, took a shower, got dressed, and called the desk to have a bellman remove my luggage.

I rejoined Ken downstairs outside the restaurant. He once again made me do all the ordering for him. When ordering, Ken would tell me what he wanted, and then make me relay it to the waiter. It had gotten beyond rude. I decided that I had had enough of it. I spoke to the waiter at length in Spanish. I asked him where he had been born, and we chit chatted about that part of Mexico, and when I had been there last, all while Ken waited fuming. The waiters had been insulted enough during the week by Ken's behavior, that they all seemed to enjoy it, and came over to the table to join in the conversation. Finally he took Ken's pancake order to the kitchen.

When the staff was outside hearing range, he looked at me coldly, and said, "I know you are seeing someone else." Of all the things I might have expected him to say, that was farthest from it. I looked at him as indignantly as possible, and said, "I don't know how you'd think I had the time to play around on you. I go to work and church, and spend the rest of my time with you. That is not the kind of person I am. Last night should have shown you that." He said, "I think the only reason you won't sleep with me is because you are afraid I'll find out that you aren't really a virgin. What's wrong, have you had the clap or something?" At that I stood up, and said, "I will have a taxi waiting to take us to the airport at 2. If you want to share the ride, you are welcome to. Until then, I really don't want to endure your presence any further."

I left the restaurant, even paying for his meal on my way out. I didn't want any of the hotel staff to have to deal with his rudeness any more than necessary. I spent the time until we left sitting on a beach chair watching the water and praying. I didn't know what God wanted of me. I had always tried to do my best. I had many flaws, but tried to live by the rules. Why was it so hard? If God really wanted me to get married, then why did he keep putting unsuitable men across my path? I knew deep down that I didn't love Ken. I was beginning to wonder if I even knew what that kind of love was.

Chapter 31: Endings

The ride to the airport was in complete silence, as was the flight home. I noticed when I tried to get up to leave the plane that my bad knee had stiffened up. By the next morning, it was swelled and warm. I recognized the signs of fluid on it. I hobbled off to work on crutches. My secretary's only response when I came in the door on crutches, was, "Looks like you had a really good time in Mexico. Here're your messages." She had seen me on crutches too many times to be concerned. I just asked her to call and get me in to see the doctor.

She fit me in right before lunch. She had the same response, and said I looked like I had fun. I told her in detail what had happened. She handed me a brochure. I didn't look at it at first because she often handed me brochures. This one was on the abusive relationships. There were 17 warning signs. I realized that Ken fit almost every one. There was a couple I couldn't answer because I didn't know if he had been raised in an abusive home. I hadn't asked, and he had never said. My doctor looked at me and said, "He flunked didn't he?" I nodded yes. She said, "You're too smart a woman to stay in that kind of relationship. How many battered women did you see at the homeless shelter? They were all at the point you are now in the beginning wondering if this guy was worth sticking with. I promise you he isn't."

"You're right. How did I let this happen? After the first time, everyone told me not to take him back, but I did anyway. Maybe I'm just not meant to marry." My doctor came around the exam table with a very large needle, and said, "I'm no expert. I've been married twice. The only thing I'm sure of is that this is going to hurt you more than it does me." At that she plunged the large needle into my knee to start draining the fluid. "You'll want to stay off this a few days, but I guess I don't have to tell you that."

That afternoon I mostly returned phone calls and dealt with the paperwork that had accumulated while I was gone. I left early to pick up the photos I had taken on the trip. When I pulled into my driveway, I was dismayed to see Ken's truck. When he saw I was on crutches, he practically carried me in the house. We looked through the pictures. He paid me for his set. His birthday was in a few days, and he wanted to know if I was going to come. I told him that I was supposed to stay off my leg. He said that if necessary he and his brother would come over and carry me to the party. I still said no. He told me that if I loved him, I would come to his birthday party no matter what. I said that if he loved me, he wouldn't put me through it. We just sort of stared at each other for a moment.

I reached into my bag, and retrieved the brochure my doctor had given me. I handed it to him. He looked at it, and he seemed to frown. I said, "Ken, I do care about you, and I think you need help. I'm willing to go to counseling with you, and stand by you all the way if you're willing to try." He just threw the brochure back at me saying that he didn't need any help. I was the one that hit him. I very calmly, trying not to escalate things, told him that until he was willing to get help, I couldn't see him any longer, but that he could call me at any time that he changed his mind. He walked to the door, turned and said, "You'll never hear from me again until you get help."

I expected him to come back to the door, but after a few minutes I heard his truck go up the street. I was so sad all of a sudden. I realized that I wasn't sad at the loss of Ken exactly, but rather at the loss of what he represented. A few days later I saw his truck over at my friend Jane's house as I drove past on my way to church. I thought about stopping but decided against it. I was expecting "I told you so's" from my friends. Instead they all seemed sorry for me, and also relieved in a way. They never liked the idea of me being with a non-Catholic. Father Paul hauled me in his office again. It was beginning to be like going to the principal's office.

His first concern was that Ken had done the damage to my knee. I told him it was just all the walking on cobble stone streets followed by a cramped airplane ride. He asked me what happened, and I told him. He looked at me very softly, and asked, "Are you telling me everything. Did he hurt you, and you know what I mean by that." I confessed to striking Ken. He laughed and said, "Good he had it coming." I said, "Father, you're not supposed to think hitting people is okay. I'm pretty sure that's a sin." He told me that I was defending myself, so it was okay. He said that's why my dad had taught me to box when I was little. Sometimes women have to defend themselves from abuse at the hands of stronger men. Then he laughed and said, "Of course, I'm not sure you've ever met a man who was stronger than you are. You didn't hurt him did you? I'd hate for him to file a grievance against you with the Bar Association."

"No, I just gave him a sore jaw to remember me by. I don't think I'm going to date again for awhile. I'm going to concentrate on my classes this fall, and maybe join a club to meet some different people, expand my horizons a bit." He came around the desk, and kissed me on the forehead and said, "I'm sorry this turned out so badly. I just think of you like a daughter, and wanted you to be happy. From now on, if you are happy spending all your free time puttering around church, I'm not going to complain."

Chapter 32: Making Choices

So for the next couple of months, I went to work, went to the courthouse and mediations, and went to church. I was taking a really hard class on contemporary issues in theology taught by the head deacon of the Archdiocese. It was very philosophical and made my head hurt. I joined the local Mensa group, and those meetings made my head hurt too. In early fall, things began to change. I kept seeing the same old truck following me. At first I thought it might be Ken driving one of his brother's work trucks, but when my secretary buzzed me with a call from the US Attorney's office, I knew. They wanted me to come in for a meeting.

At least I had made enough trips now that I didn't get lost on the way anymore. I was told very quickly that they had decided to convene a grand jury to begin an investigation into Davidson's activities at his farm. They wanted to go over with me again certain specific things. They especially wanted to know if I had seen or talked to anyone who seemed to be from a foreign country. The first person was of course the Colonel's right hand man. I told them that he seemed to have kind of a German accent. They pulled out a file, put a set of six photos in front of me, and asked if any of those men were the man I was talking about. I picked him out right away. They made me sign my name to the back of the photograph.

They questioned me for 4 hours with only a couple of short breaks. At the end, I was exhausted. I think they were too. Before I left, they asked me to come with them into another office. It was a large office, but empty. I sat down in the chair by the desk, and in about 10 minutes an older man entered the room. He introduced himself as the Assistant US Attorney for our district. He was the man who was going to handle the grand jury, and any potential prosecutions. He was very direct. He said he wanted me in protective custody immediately. I told him I wasn't going back to that seedy hotel. He said, "You've misunderstood me. I'm not talking about a few days. I'm talking about permanent relocation. We want you to go into witness protection."

"You've got to be kidding. I'm not going into witness protection. I have a home, a practice, family and friends. You can't possibly expect me to just walk from my life." I guess I had raised my voice a bit too loud because one of the marshals came into the room. He just waved the marshal back out the door. After the marshal had left, he said, "I'm not making this request lightly. I can't force you obviously. Normally when we offer witness protection it is to someone under indictment for something, so they are pretty eager to take it. I understand how huge this is. You'd never be able to practice law again. You'd never be able to see your friends and family again. We would make every attempt to place you somewhere nice. I really think you should let us protect you."

I couldn't believe what I was hearing. It had to be a joke. Something wasn't right. Finally I asked, "Why now? What has happened?" He seemed really uncomfortable with my question. Reluctantly he said, "Bob Jeffries is dead. He died in a very suspicious farm accident. We have reason to believe that someone involved with Bill Davidson had something to do with it." The room started to spin. I must have gone completely pale because he hit a buzzer, and one of the marshals came in the room and they helped me over to a couch. I had to sit with my head between my knees for several minutes to clear my head.

Bob Jeffries was the farmer I had manipulated into getting me an invitation to the Colonel's meeting. Now he was dead, and I couldn't help but feel responsible. All I could repeat over and over again was that it was my fault. When they were finally able to get my attention, they told me that it wasn't my fault. Mr. Jeffries had agreed to testify before the grand jury. He died two days later. He said, "There is a possibility that it was suicide. He did not want to testify, but we agree to get the FmHA to make some concessions on his loans. We were putting a lot of pressure on him, and I know Davidson's people were too. You shouldn't blame yourself, but you can understand why we want you protected. You are the only witness we have that isn't under some kind of cloud. You can testify with clean hands."

I looked up from between my knees and said, "Testify about what? I understood the fraud case, but I never saw anything criminal at his farm. Strange stuff, but nothing criminal." He replied, "You saw more than you realize, but I can't explain to you what that was at this time. It can't seem as if I have influenced your testimony. You're going to have to just trust me." I stood up a bit shaky, but resolute, and said, "I'm going home. I'm going to pray about this, and I will let you know later what I have decided." I walked out of his office, and didn't look back.

Chapter 33: The Hardest Confession

I drove over to church. It was after office hours, but I just hoped he was home. I rang the bell, heard his dog bark, and eventually heard someone coming to the door. When he opened the door, he laughed, and said, "What are you doing here? I thought you were someone looking for a handout. You're not here for gas money or something, are you?" All I could say was, "I need to go to confession immediately." His face fell, and he said, "What's happened? Come inside where we can talk." I walked back towards his living room, and sat down on the couch. When he came into the room, I just blurted out, "I think I've killed a man." Fr. Paul kind of dropped into his recliner. He asked, "Did you have a wreck? Did you hit someone?"

I told him what I had found out from the feds. He got up, and came across and sat next to me. I had to put my head between my knees again, and started to feel really sick. I grabbed his waste basket, and started throwing up in it. All he could do was rub his hand across my back until I quit being sick. I finally had nothing left on my stomach, but started to hyperventilate. He got up and got a paper bag for me to breathe into. He told me to calm to down that it was going to be okay. All I could say was, "How is it going to be okay? I'm responsible for a man's death." He got quite cross with me at that point. He told me that I was not responsible for Mr. Jeffries' death. He refused to give me absolution for it.

Once I regained my composure, he said, "You're going to have to go into witness protection. None of us would survive well seeing something happen to you." All I could say was no. At that moment, I was determined that I was not going to run and hide. "Bob Jeffries was good man, a pretty good farmer, and had lots of people that cared about him. He didn't run away. If I run away, it would just make it that much easier for Davidson to intimidate the next person after me." He inhaled, and nodded his head. We said a rosary together for Bob's soul. He gave me such a long hug as I left, that I wondered if he was ever going to let me go.

A week after my last meeting with the feds, I got a call from a local drug store. They said my photos were ready to be picked up. I couldn't remember taking a roll of film in, but I was always taking pictures of things, so I figured I must have taken them in and forgotten to pick them up. I drove right past the place on my way to the office, so I just ran in the next morning on my way to work. I paid for them, and threw them in my bag. I didn't think anything else about them until mid morning. I had hit the office running that morning with some important paperwork that needed to be finished immediately.

When I finally had a breather, I remembered about the photos, and pulled the envelope out. I looked at the first two really puzzled, and then the realization of what I was looking at hit me all at once. The room began to spin again. I just did find my chair. I dropped the photos and they scattered all across my desk. I was looking at pictures of myself with a variety of people in my life. There was a picture of Oma and I in front of the rectory, and a picture of me and my mom going into the VFW for a meeting. There were pictures of me with a variety of different people, my secretary at a diner downtown, an old college roommate having coffee, and even clients going into the courthouse. The last picture was of Fr. Paul giving me a goodbye hug on his porch the night I found out about Bob's death.

I knew immediately what this meant. I was being followed, and they were paying attention to my friends and family now. I called the feds. They sent an agent over to escort me downtown to the Murrah Building. I met with the female investigator who first approached me all those months ago. She looked through the photos, and asked if I had noticed anyone taking the pictures. I replied that I had felt followed at times, but never saw anyone actually taking pictures. She said as grainy as they were, they were probably taken from a great distance, so that's not surprising.

She again requested that I enter witness protection. "It is obvious that you have no concern for you own well being, but surely you care about the people around you?" I had never once thought that my being in danger might put anyone else in danger. I left her office and walked next door to St. Joseph's. It was just time for the noon mass to be finished. I sat in the back as people walked out past me. It was a beautiful old church. My older brothers had gone to school here in the late '50's. When the school closed in the middle '60's, the school land was sold to the government for the Federal Building. I often liked to just sit in the old church when I was doing business downtown. It was quiet, and the stained glass windows were exquisite. My dad used to sit here on his lunch hour when stuck on jury duty.

      Churches had always been second homes to me. As I sat there and thought about the events of that year, I knew it wasn't a game anymore. I couldn't stand the idea that people I loved and cared about might get hurt because of me. By the time the priest came up to tell me he needed to lock up the church, I had a plan. I walked back next door, and asked to see the agent again. I had to wait several minutes, but when I was finally brought back to her office, I told her that I needed their help. She thought I meant witness protection, and I told her that I still refused to run and hide, but I needed to protect the people closest to me. She was confused by what I meant. I told her I wanted their help to move. I was going to separate myself immediately from the people I cared about most in my life.

Chapter 34: Farewells

I knew if I discussed my plans with people, it would just scare them. Within days, I made arrangements to move from the east side of the metro area, to the far western side to a rural bedroom community. I'm still not sure how everything was ultimately arranged, but I was very quickly and quietly moved. I isolated myself from the friends I had leaned on so heavily. I suspect at a subconscious level they may have even been relieved. I began attending a new church, and tried very hard to not make new friends. I did join the choir, but it was a much larger church, so I easily got lost in the crowd.

The week I made the move coincided with Fr. Paul's vacation. He came back to find me gone, and removed from the music ministry calendar, and a new president of the women's group already installed. He called a few times, but I had my secretary tell him I was out. I completely isolated myself. I knew they didn't understand, but I just couldn't stand thinking about anyone else being hurt because of me.

My old church always scheduled a Christmas party, after the holidays. We were usually so busy preparing for the holidays before hand, that it wasn't practical before then. It was a great way to thank people who helped out around church later in January when everyone's lives had settled back down. I got an invitation. I wanted to go so badly, but I thought that if I saw everyone again, I'd just lose it. I had to RSVP because it was being catered. I called the secretary, and she put me on hold very quickly as if she had someone on the other line. When the phone picked up again, it was Fr. Paul on the other end.

His voice was curt, "I understand you waited until I was out of town to pull up stakes, and leave without so much as a goodbye. I'd like you to explain yourself please." My deepest desire was to lie to him. I wanted to make him angry enough that he'd never think of me again. I couldn't bring myself to even speak. I guess he sensed something was seriously wrong. He asked, "Where are you right now." I told him at the office. He told me to meet him at the Classen Grill at

2pm. We had eaten there before when he had been downtown at the Cathedral for some function. It was just up the street from my office. 2 o'clock would save us from the lunch rush.

I parked on the west side, and went inside the Grill. He was already there at a table in the corner. He had started on a plate of Classen potatoes. They were a signature dish, kind of fried garlic mashed potato balls. As I slinked into the seat across from him, he said, "I started without you because I had a feeling I wouldn't get to eat otherwise. So are you going to tell me finally what's going on? People are whispering that you left because we had a fight."

I looked at him, trying very hard to lie. I told him that I got evicted because my dog barked too much. I had to move quickly, and was too embarrassed to tell anyone. He continued to eat in silence, and then finally said, "For a lawyer, you're a really bad liar. You want to try again?" I resigned myself to it, and dug in my bag for the photos. I laid them out on the table. He saw pictures of me and Oma, and he and I at the church picnic months before. At first he didn't understand what I was showing him, and then he said, "You're in all these pictures."

I had been a photographer since my early teens. One of the first things I bought with my first paychecks from my movie theater job was an expensive Minolta. I had served as yearbook and newspaper photographer in high school. I had made money in college doing party pictures at frat house events and weddings. I had always been the official photographer for family functions, holidays and church events. Being the photographer meant that there have actually been very few pictures taken over the years that I am also in the frame.

He asked, "Who took these?" I replied, "Who do you think. My grand jury testimony will be in a couple of months. They are trying to intimidate me any way they can. I don't want anyone else hurt." Fr. Paul sighed heavily, leaned back against the booth and looked out the window towards the expressway. Finally he turned and said, "I'm saddened that you didn't come and talk to me about this. I'm not a child. I served in World War II, maybe not as distinguished as your father's service, but I did serve. I understand your wanting to protect everyone, but when people love and care about you, you don't have the right to treat them this way. What is the difference between taking witness protection, and just cutting everyone out of your life? At least with witness protection we'd know you were safe." I replied that the difference is that I can still have the hope that someday I will get my life back the way it was. Entering witness protection was admitting that I had lost it forever. I'd never be able to call anyone or even just send a Christmas card.

"Catherine, the life you had is over. Whether you want to admit it to yourself or not, you can't go back. The genie is out of the bottle. There comes a time in everyone's life when that happens. You can't have everything you want, no one can. I also know that trying to change your mind once you've made it up is impossible. The only thing I ask is that you come to the party. I obviously can't break your confidence to tell people what has happened. That's up to you. It may seem silly, but people need a chance to say goodbye." I agreed. I knew it would be hard to see everyone, but I missed them.

Chapter 35: One Last Christmas

The party was the third week in January. I'm normally early to everything I go to. I decided to be a little fashionably late for once. I didn't want any extra time for people to corner me. I just drove around killing time through my old neighborhood. Finally, I felt like it was time to make my appearance. I tried to quietly slip in and find a seat. That idea lasted about 10 seconds. Oma saw me come in, and ran over from where she was messing with the buffet table to give me a big hug. I'd only been gone 2 months, but people acted like it had been years. I tried very hard to keep my composure.

People seemed to accept the story that I had been evicted because of my dog. There was a couple that looked at me funny. I realized later that they knew that I had owned my home, so the story seemed silly to them. Oma knew it too, but she acted like there was nothing wrong. To this day, I don't know if Fr. Paul told her what was really going on or not. I just tried very hard to put it all behind me so I could enjoy the party. I tried hard not to think about the fact that it would be my last.

The music director started playing Christmas carols on the piano in the parish hall, and several people shoved me up to sing. I think it might have been my best rendition of Little Drummer Boy ever. When Father Paul got up towards the end to recognize the different people who did all the different ministries around the church, I was grateful that he didn't seem to be mentioning me for any of the ones I had been involved in. I wasn't involved in them anymore, so that just made sense. Just before he was to sit down, he said, "Oh yes, one last thing. There's a woman who breezed into our lives a few years ago after coming home from college. She has just as quickly breezed back out. I have a special present for her, for all the work she has done for our parish, with extreme gratitude."

Everyone in the room knew he was talking about me without mentioning my name. I got up quickly, hoping to take the spotlight off of myself as quickly as possible. As I made my way to the front in between the tables, people kept patting me as I went by them. I eventually made it to the front. Fr. Paul handed me a small box, and gave me a big hug. Everyone clapped, and I tried to quickly return to my seat. I went back through the gauntlet. The rest of the evening went quickly, and I tried to lose myself in the crowd as the throng exited.

    I was just putting my keys in my car door, when I felt a hand on my shoulder. It was our parish's Deacon. He was a simple man, but a really good one. We had never been particularly close. We didn't have much in common. All he said was, "I didn't get my goodbye hug." I gave him a hug, and he turned and walked away without another word. I couldn't remember ever hugging him before. I've often wondered if Fr. Paul might have told him what was going on with me, or if he just missed having me around. I never got the chance to ask him.

    I sat in my car for a moment, and then opened the box Father Paul had given me. Inside was a small golden crucifix. It was weathered with age and a bit tarnished. Christ's face was almost worn smooth. There was a small note with it that said, "This cross was on the rosary my grandmother gave me when I left for boot camp. It has long since fallen apart, but I thought maybe you could make a new rosary using it." Months later I dug around and found a rosary center to match it that I had gotten on my last long trip to Mexico. It had Our Lady of Guadalupe on it, and reminded me of my Godmother. It made a beautiful golden rosary that I carry to this day everywhere I go.

Chapter 36: A Last Walk Around the Lake

Shortly after I moved, I had taken in a roommate. I guess I found myself so lonely in my new isolation, that I needed some kind of human contact. I told myself that the extra income would help as well. I also liked the idea that my dog would have someone around during the day. She had been hurt on the job, and had a breakdown after having neck surgery. Someone I had worked with at the mental health clinic I volunteered at had asked me if I had room for a boarder because she was going to be homeless.

She stayed for a couple of weeks. It did seem strange to have someone in my home. I had roommates all during college, and had been legal guardian for a teenage nephew for several years off and on, so I wasn't unfamiliar with sharing space. It had just been a long time. I realized later that I hadn't asked very many questions about her before opening up my home. A few weeks after she moved in I found out that she had two small sons, one just 16 months old. The infant was being cared for by her ex-husband and his new wife, and her 4 year old son by a different father was staying with her mother.

She hadn't gotten to see them regularly because both lived several hours away. I came home on Tuesday the 12th to find a note that she had gone to visit them. I'm embarrassed to say that I looked around to make sure she hadn't stolen anything. I guess somewhere along the way I had gotten cynical on top of everything else. When I was satisfied that everything was where it should be, I just relaxed. I guess I had finally settled into my new living arrangements. It did seem strange to not have anywhere to go to at night. I had gotten so used to having meetings and functions over the years.

That's when I remembered that I wasn't entirely alone. Buster had jumped up on the couch and placed his head in my lap. He wasn't going to sleep though. He was eagerly wagging his tail. I knew what he wanted. We had moved next to a large lake, and he loved going exploring. Sometimes he liked it so much, that he went without me. Bassets are very good diggers.

I just looked at him, and asked if he wanted to go for a walk. At the word "walk" he got very excited, jumped down, and ran to the front door.

We spent the next hour walking along the lake shore. It was so peaceful. I got to watch the sun set over the water from the spillway. A couple of fishermen were trying to catch catfish off the dam. I waived back at one that had waived at me. I remember thinking that he must have been one of my new neighbors. I tried very hard to keep Buster away from any flotsam on the shore. He had the disgusting habit of rubbing his face on dead washed up fish. I never understood that one.

We eventually made our way back home. I went to bed early and just read a book. It had been a long time since I had allowed myself to do that. I guess I started to believe that things had calmed down. I no longer felt like I was being followed. I went to sleep that night thinking that I had turned a corner. In the morning I didn't go to the office because I had a mediation scheduled in a small town courthouse 2 hours away. I got an early start, had the mediation finished by noon, and spent my lunch time roaming through some small antique shops in the town square.

I found a piece of crystal that matched my mother's. She was always on the look out for extra pieces. It was expensive, but a fair price for such a rare platter. I decided it would make a nice Valentine's gift for her. She was big on holidays, in a way I just didn't feel anymore. It was as if holidays just didn't seem the same without my dad being there. I wondered if I would ever get over the grief of his passing. My mother had a boyfriend that everyone in the family universally despised, but I tried very hard to tolerate.

No matter how upset at my mother I would get, deep down, I knew that my father wouldn't want me to act that way. If nothing else, I always knew he had loved her. I went by her place on my way back to the office that afternoon, and gave her the present. She invited me to a Valentine's party at the VFW post. She was always trying to fix me up, and I guess this was another attempt. I reminded her that I had a class the next evening, and begged off. I didn't stay long. I hadn't been to the VFW since moving. I was trying to stay away from my usual haunts.

When I came in that night, I had several hang-ups on my answering machine. I got very few calls at home since moving and changing my number. I decided that it was probably just a wrong number. In the back of my mind, I had the idea that maybe it was Ken trying to reach out to me again. I never found out.

Chapter 37: On A Clear Day

That Thursday morning started like any other. The alarm went off; I took a shower, and packed my lunch and dinner to go while eating dry toast for breakfast. I wore an ordinary pair of dress pants and a red golf shirt to work because I knew I wouldn't have to go to court that day. I tried to avoid trips either to the courthouse or out of town on days when I had class. I was taking a class that semester from a professor I really liked, so I wanted to focus my attention. My office was half way to the Pastoral Center where the classes were held, so I found it easier to stay late at the office to eat dinner at my desk before heading off to class. I grabbed my briefcase and kissed my dog goodbye, not realizing that I wouldn't be home that night.

I spent the morning working on a report for the Agriculture Department, and returning phone calls. The weather had been warm that week, but it was a little cold as I entered the building that morning. I was hoping it was going to warm up some that afternoon so that I could shoot a few baskets at the Pastoral Center before my class started. I mostly remember that day as being very ordinary. If I had known how my life was preparing to change in such a drastic way, I would have stopped and looked around, and paid more attention.

I have lost the last 30 to 60 minutes before I left that day. I suspect they are gone forever. Since I was by myself, I've got no one to ask. The very next thing I remember after the gap in my memory is putting the key in my office door on my way out. I had just put my briefcase down to pull the door shut, when I felt something move next to my right shoulder. As I turned that direction, I heard a man's voice shout, "An eye for an eye saith the Lord!"

My glasses went flying through the air, and I felt an intense pain above my right eye, and realized that blood was now flowing into my eye. I was stunned, and without my glasses, I couldn't see who had just attacked me. He screamed at me, "This is for the Colonel you bitch." I saw a blurry image coming at my face again, but was able to get my left arm up to protect my face. I felt another sharp pain on my left wrist and then right hand. I pushed forward with my left arm ahead of me, and slammed my attacker against the wall to the left of the office door. I heard him moan in pain. With my left arm across his chest, I began to punch at the man with my right fist remembering everything my father had taught me. After several jabs, I cut my knuckles on what I realized later must have been braces on his teeth. When I drew my hand back in pain, that moment of hesitation gave him the opportunity to grab my neck. I grabbed his collar and slammed him into the wall again. I brought my knee up hard to where I knew his stomach was. I heard him exhale as if I had knocked the wind out of him. He slid down the wall, coming to rest on the floor.

    I stopped hitting him. I thought he had had enough. I heard myself scream, "What the hell is your problem? What do you want?" I tried to look around for my glasses as I wiped the blood flowing across my face. Between rasps, I heard him say, "You betrayed your race. You sided with the Jew government. You deserve to pay for your betrayal." As he said betrayal, he lunged at me again, and I realized too late that I was standing with my back to the top of the marble staircase. As I began to brace myself against his renewed attack, I felt myself falling backwards into oblivion.

Chapter 38: The Other Side of the Mirror

I remember only snippets of the next several hours. I know that going down the stairs backwards, head first caused a head injury, a back injury, dislocated my right shoulder, destroyed the ACL in my left knee, and broke my left big toe. I must have become entangled in the wrought iron railing at some point. I do remember flashes of light and dark that must correspond to when my body was facing the overhead lights or turned away as I tumbled down. I remember coming to a stop at the bottom of the stairs. My attacker apparently raced down the stairs after me. He had picked up his dropped weapon and was pointing it at me when I looked up. He said, "Repent of your sins, and I will spare your life." When I didn't respond, he stepped on my damaged right shoulder and screamed, "Do you want to burn in the crimson fire?! You have been judged by the brotherhood." I found the breath to scream back at him, "My only judge is Jesus Christ." At that, he became enraged, pulled his hand back, and I knew he was going to stab me again.

He was still standing with his foot on my shoulder, but dropped down to his knee. I got my left hand up just in time to take the stab to the middle of my palm. I felt the sharpness of the metal go in, but it didn't hurt at first. Then in a moment like a bright light, it hit me like a long inhale. It was as if at that moment I began to feel all my injuries at once. It was like being hit by a strong wave that knocks you down. I couldn't breathe. I couldn't cry. I began to tremble. I could hear my father's voice telling me to pray. I began saying the Hail Mary. I said the first half but couldn't seem to remember the second half. I just kept repeating the first half of the prayer over and over again.

He began to pace back and forth at the foot of the stairs. At first he was muttering to himself, and then he started screaming for me to shut up. Finally, at the top of his lungs he screamed, "Idol Worshipper!!" He dropped down on top of me and grabbed my neck again. He alternately strangled my neck and slammed my head into the marble, all the while screaming that I was an idol worshipper and a papist. Darkness started to close in on my vision. His voice started to sound muffled and far away. I could hear myself say, "please don't hurt me," and as I felt the darkness surround me, I finally remembered the end of the prayer. My father told me once that if you don't have time to finish a prayer on this side you can finish it on the other side. I thought I had crossed over. The next thing I remember is the sound of a vacuum cleaner.

Chapter 39: Humpty Dumpty

The vacuum seemed to be coming closer or maybe I was just able to hear it better as I was regaining consciousness. All of a sudden, the vacuum stopped, and I heard a woman scream, "Madre de Dios." I felt a hand on the side of my face. I tried to speak, but it was like the words would not come out. I could taste blood. I heard the woman run up the hallway. What seemed like an eternity later I heard footsteps, someone touching my arm, and telling me not to move. Then I heard sirens approaching. The next thing I remember was a jolt as I was being loaded in the ambulance. I heard someone tell me to try to stay still. I could only see the roof of the ambulance. I couldn't move any part of my body. I was strapped down. I could feel someone tapping the back of my right hand. I heard him say, "I'm going to try to start another line."

I heard the siren silence, and then the ambulance bounced to a stop. I felt the rush of cool air as the doors opened, and another jolt as they slid me out. All I could see was the overhead fluorescent lights quickly alternating with ceiling tiles. When I came to a stop, I could hear all sorts of activity around me. I saw a bright light in my eyes and someone asked me what my name was. I didn't hear myself say anything. I heard the doctor turn and ask one of the paramedics if I had said anything. The paramedic said that I had been in and out, mostly out.

The next thing I remember is hearing a different voice say, "Ma'am, can you tell me what happened to you? Do you know who did this to you?" I didn't hear myself answer him. Finally, he turned to the nurse and said, "Do you have any ID on her?" The nurse said, "The EMT's brought her briefcase in." I heard the familiar sound of the straps on my briefcase being opened, and the sound of papers being rustled, and then the sound of Velcro being opened. The next thing I heard was the detective saying, "Oh my God."

Chapter 40: Kaleidoscope

All of a sudden, my view of the ceiling was obscured by a vaguely familiar face. I heard him say, "Cath, is that you? Oh My God. What happened? Who did this to you? Oh my God, Oh my God, I promise we will get this guy." His face disappeared, and I heard him ask the nurse for a phone. A few minutes or a few hours later, I had no conception of time, he came back. He touched my arm and leaned in close to my ear. He whispered, "Cath, I just talked to the doctor, and he said you hadn't been violated. I don't want you worrying about that. I called Father Paul. Is there anyone else I can call for you?" I heard myself say no. Then I realized that it was Dan I was talking to, a friend from the Archdiocesan Choir. I had forgotten he was a policeman.

    I heard myself say, "Dan, is that you? How's your wife?" I don't remember hearing an answer. The next thing I remember is hearing someone plod into the room out of breath. I felt a hand gently touch my face. I heard someone start to cry. I tried to reach my right hand out, but still couldn't move it. He must have seen me try to move my hand because he grasped my finger tips in his hand very gingerly. My arm was tied to a board, so all I could do was squeeze his fingers. When I did, he leaned down and kissed the back of my hand. I thought for a minute that it was my Dad, but he'd been dead for many years.

    I heard someone else come into the room. It must have been a nurse, because the person holding my hand stood up, and shrieked at her, "Why haven't you cleaned her up yet? Don't you know who this is? I can't anoint her forehead if it's covered with blood." I realized then that it must be Father Paul in the room with me. She said they were waiting to remove the head restraint after reading the X-rays to make sure my neck was okay. He said, "You mean she could be paralyzed?" The nurse responded that she could only give that kind of information to my next of kin. Father Paul said, "I am her next of kin."

Chapter 41: A Light in the Darkness

Father Paul told me later that all he could look at was my eye where the large gash was. He said that eye was looking towards my right ear. He decided that he couldn't wait any longer. He thought I was going to die. He began to give me the Anointing of the Sick. I heard him unzip some kind of case, and then he began to pray, "Through this holy anointing, may the Lord in his love and mercy help you with the grace of the Holy Spirit." I felt the oil run down my forehead, and then his hand touched it so gently. I felt a warmth overtake me. Something happened that I can't explain. Father Paul stroked my hair and said my name, and began to cry again. He told me later that he had used too much oil because his hands were shaking, and when the oil ran into the wound above my eye, that my eye snapped back into place and he could tell that I was trying to focus it on him.

When he had regained his composure, he went to anoint my hand. My right hand was still strapped down because there was an IV inserted into the back of it. He walked around to the other side of the bed, touched my left hand, and exclaimed, "Jesus, Mary and Joseph, what is this?" The weapon that had stabbed my left palm was still embedded. The EMT's didn't want to remove it in the field, so they taped gauze around it to immobilize it. The nurse explained this to us, and assured us that it wasn't bleeding any longer, and that they had a surgical resident coming in to remove it to minimize any potential nerve or tendon damage.

He touched the inside tip of my middle finger that was sticking up above the bandages and said, "May the Lord who frees you from sin save you and raise you up." He asked the nurse if she could leave the room for a moment. Then he rolled the stool up close to the bed and whispered in my left ear, "Catherine can you understand me?" I said yes, and he said, "Do you understand that you have been severely injured, and there is a chance that you might not make it?" I said, "Yes sir." He asked if I wanted to make a confession. I tried to think of a lifetime of wrongs I might have committed and forgotten to confess. I told him about being angry with my mother, saying a few too many cuss words, being arrogant, short tempered, wasteful and not as attentive to my prayers as I should have been. He stroked my hair again, and asked if I was sure that was all I wanted to confess, that I knew I could tell him anything. I told him that I had also been very angry at God for taking my father away from me. He touched my head again and said, "May God grant you pardon and peace. I absolve you from all your sins, in the name of the Father, Son and Holy Spirit." I felt myself drift off again.

It seemed such a long time. I still do not know if it was minutes or hours. It was probably minutes. I awoke to the sound of some mumbling in the hall way, and two nurses came in and began to cut the white tape that was across my head. It was as if they were unwrapping a very large Christmas present. The foam blocks that had been surrounding my head had been very hot. The sides of my face were covered in sweat that turned cold when the air in the room hit them. I heard the sound of Velcro again as they removed the brace around my neck. Almost immediately, I heard one of the nurses sharply inhale and say, "Wow, look at those bruises. We'd better get a picture." It was described to me later that there was a definitive set of hand shaped bruises around my neck.

Sometime later, a doctor entered the room and injected something into my left arm and above my right eye to deaden the areas. After he stitched up the wound above my eye, he eventually began to cut away the tape and gauze surrounding my hand. When it was clear, he said, "It looks like some kind of tool." He draped a green cloth over my arm, and painted something orange and cold over my hand. Father Paul asked him to be very careful because I was a musician. The doctor looked at me smiling, and asked what instrument I played. I told him guitar and mandolin. He continued to smile, but had the faintest crease appear in his forehead. He said, "Well, I'll take it very easy, don't worry."

Even though my hand was numb and no longer hurt, I could still feel a kind of pressure as he removed the thing. He put it into a steel basin at the foot of the bed. He said, "It looks like a wood carving tool of some kind. I don't think it got the nerve, but I'm going to be very careful stitching it up. I'll use very small stitches, and it's just ragged enough to really knit well." He removed and replaced the small bandages covering the score of defensive wounds on my arms and wrists, explaining that they weren't going to need stitches. About the time he was finished with the smaller wounds, a policeman in uniform came in the room to get the steel basin. The doctor asked him what he thought, and the policeman said, "I don't know. If there were any prints, I think the tape may have ruined them. We'll see what we can do with it."

Chapter 42: The Bruises on the Wall

Shortly after that, Dan came back into the room. He said something quietly to Father Paul, who said, "She's been in and out, but she is talking now." Dan walked over to the bed, and said, "You look better than the last time I saw you. Listen, I've had the lab guys all over your building, the stairs and the atrium. We haven't found anything useful yet. The cleaning lady who found you must have been an illegal because she disappeared as soon as the ambulance got there. I've been able to keep the press out for now. If you let me put it down on my report as an attempted sexual assault, it will keep your name out of the paper. As far as my boss will ever know, the cleaning lady just interrupted him. If we catch him, he's going down for attempted murder. The pictures of the bruises around your neck are all the evidence we'll need. The doctor said that if you didn't have such strong neck muscles, you'd be dead."

One of the other doctors came in to talk to me. He said that all the X-rays had come back negative, but he was concerned about my loss of consciousness. He wanted to know if I had ever had a concussion before. I told him that I had had several over the years. I had a really bad one as a teenager when I fell off the top of a box car while at summer camp and had been unconscious for over 30 minutes. He said my inner cranial pressure was okay, and he didn't think I had a brain bleed, but a very serious concussion. He said I had a lot of soft tissue injuries. My knee was swollen and discolored as was my shoulder. He explained about how they had "reduced" my shoulder. They had put it back into place, and then taken a second set of X-rays to make sure it was okay.

I didn't remember any of the X-rays being taken. Since they had cleared my spine, and knew I hadn't fractured any vertebra, he wanted to roll me over because I seemed to be guarding my right side. I couldn't roll over. I wasn't paralyzed, but it was as if the muscles just wouldn't respond. He asked one of the nurses to help him try to roll me onto my left side. When he touched my lower right side, I screamed in pain. He moved his hand higher, and I could tolerate it. They rolled me towards the side of the bed where Father Paul was still sitting. There was a silence. I could see concern on Father Paul's face, and he got up quickly to go around the bed to look too. I heard him inhale sharply, but all I could think of was that he was looking at my bare backside. Telling him my sins was one thing, this was entirely different.

They very gently rolled me back down. The doctor asked the nurse if I had been passing blood in my urine. She said no. He looked at me and said, "You have a very large bruise on your back. My first concern is that you might have damage to one or both of your kidneys, but if you aren't passing blood, it is more likely more soft tissue damage. I have a neurologist coming to see you in a few minutes, and I'm going to ask him to assess the strength and feeling you have below the bruise, okay? I'll be back later to see you. You're in good hands."

After the doctor left us alone, I seemed to realize for the first time that I didn't have any clothes on. I looked at him and said, "Father, I don't have any clothes on. Where are my clothes?" He kind of sat upright but didn't really look at me as he answered, "Catherine you've been around hospitals enough to know that they have to cut your clothes off in order to help you. It's okay for doctors and nurses to see you that way. The police took your clothes away. All of your other things are here, and I'll take care of them for you." I asked him why the police took my clothes. He looked at me with a puzzled expression. "Catherine, do you remember what happened to you?" I told him no. He said, "You were attacked outside your office and thrown down the stairs. You are bruised and battered, and have a bad concussion, but you're going to be fine. You've got no broken bones."

I tried very hard to remember what had happened. I wouldn't remember any part of the attack for months. My mind had become like a vinyl record that had a bunch of scratches. Every time I thought I was remembering something, all of a sudden, my mind would skip. I looked at Father Paul and asked him who had attacked me. He said, "We don't know yet. The police are trying to find out. Do you remember anything about the man?" I felt a cold chill go down my spine. I whispered, "I was attacked by a man? Was I assaulted?" He reached up to rub my forearm, "No, you weren't violated like that. Put that out of your mind. Catherine, I want you to listen to me, this was not your fault. Had anything happened, it would not have compromised you. It is his sin, not yours. When they were evaluating you in the emergency room, that is one of the things they looked at for the police, and you were not molested in any way. You've just been hurt so very badly, but it will all heal with time."

  A few minutes later another doctor entered the room. He introduced himself, and asked the nurse who came in with him to raise the head of the bed. He explained that he was going to test both my mental status and motor skills. That was the best way to figure out what might be going on in my head. He said ideally he'd like to use the new Cat-Scan machine, but it wasn't working, and they weren't sure when it was going to be repaired. He asked me some basic questions about where I was, what day it was, those kinds of things. I seemed to be able to answer all of those questions, but couldn't answer any questions about what had happened to me. He gave me a list of things to remember, and then asked me something else. When he came back to the list to see how much I remembered, I could only remember a few items on the list, and not in the correct order. He began to write on his clip board. He asked me if I spoke any foreign languages, and Father Paul piped up that I spoke three languages. He asked me to say something in Spanish. I couldn't. It was as if that part was just gone. I became very agitated. They tried to calm me down. I almost pulled my IV loose in the process.

  Once I calmed down, they went on to some other tests. He shined a flashlight in my eyes off and on. He stuck a tongue depressor in my mouth to see if I could gag. I almost threw up. He ran the depressor over my tongue and lips. He ran a wheel across my cheek and down my neck. My neck was very sore to the touch. He even had me smell some little vials, and seemed to be testing my hearing. After testing my right ear, I noticed that he wrote something down on his clipboard. He rolled the little wheel across the bottom of my feet, and then started sticking pins in my skin at various places. I felt every prick except for the outside of my right thigh. That seemed to be kind of numb. I could feel the pressure, but it didn't hurt like at the other places.

He also had me do a bunch of tests that reminded me of a field sobriety test. I had to touch my nose, which was kind of hard with one arm taped to a board, and the other wrapped in a dressing. Finally after poking and prodding me pretty much all over, they lowered the bed back down, and he asked me to roll over. I still could not make myself roll over. He again had the nurse help me roll onto my left side. The doctor kind of whistled. He said, "Wow, that's impressive. That looks like you got kicked by a horse. Well, I guess if you can't roll over, I'm not going to ask you to stand up and walk for me. I'd like to see how straight you can walk, but I understand that you have an injured knee, so we'll save that for another day.

I wanted to ask him a million questions, but was afraid to. Father Paul wasn't. He piped right up and asked if I was going to be okay. The doctor said he wanted to review the X-rays again, and talk to his attending, and then he'd come back. I don't remember ever seeing him again. I just remember being very tired. I told Father Paul that I wanted to sleep. He said he didn't know if I should or not. He went and asked the nurse, and she said it was okay, that they would be watching me. For some reason, I noticed for the first time that I was no longer in the ER. I was in a room with windows along one side with what looked like a desk on the other side of it. Two people were sitting at the desk. It looked like the room my father died in. I realized I was in the ICU. I didn't remember being moved. I started to wonder what time it was.

I turned and looked the other way towards where Father Paul was sitting, and asked him how long I had been there. He said I shouldn't worry about that right now, that I should just rest. I looked at him almost crying, and said, "Please." He looked down at his feet, and said that I had been there over 10 hours. He told me it was after 4am. I started to cry almost uncontrollably. He tried calming me down by rubbing my upper arm. Some monitor started to beep, and the nurse came in. She had a syringe, and injected it into my IV line. I felt a sting in my hand as it went in. I could almost feel the sedative go up my arm. As I was drifting off, I heard the nurse say to Father Paul that agitation was common with head injuries.

Chapter 43: Dawn of a New Day

I seemed to be dreaming about being on a beach. I awoke to the feeling of the warm sun on my face. I wasn't sure where I was at first. The sun was shining in my face through the window. I started to reach for my nightstand to put my glasses on, but my left hand hit something. That's when I saw the bed rail. I wasn't in my own bed at all. Someone was sitting next to me with his head resting on the bed next to my left knee. As I was waking up, I realized that I was very uncomfortable. I hated sleeping on my back. I only did that in hospitals. My first thought was where am I? I saw some movement to my right. I could see someone coming into the room, but without my glasses, I couldn't tell who they were. A woman came up to the bed, and started to take my blood pressure, and stuck a thermometer in my mouth. These were so familiar.

She asked me how I was feeling. I didn't answer her because of the thermometer. When she ripped the blood pressure cup off, the sound of the ripping Velcro stirred awake the person sitting next to me. She looked at him, and asked if she could get him anything. He said a younger back, and the nurse laughed and said that they could all use one of those. I recognized his voice. I wondered what he was doing here. I wondered what I was doing here. I tried to shift myself around in the bed to get more comfortable. All of a sudden I felt a shooting pain in my back that went down my right side almost to my toes. It was as if the pain snapped me back to reality. I remembered where I was. Father Paul had stood up, and was standing and stretching next to the head of the bed. He brushed the hair off my forehead, and asked me how I was feeling.

I told him I wasn't very comfortable. He laughed and told me that if I was starting to complain, then I must be feeling better. He squeezed the fingers on my left hand and told me that he needed to go down the hall, but would be back in a little while. In the meantime, the nurse had come back in the room, and seemed to be changing the IV bag behind my head. She then went to the end of the bed, flipped up the blanket on the right side, and unhooked a different kind of bag that was clipped to the side of the bed. She turned to me and said, "Fluid in and fluid out," then left the room. She hadn't flipped the edge of the blanket back down, and I could see a tube coming off the bag snaking back under the blanket up my right leg. I realized what it was, a catheter. Now every time I moved, I felt the additional discomfort of having tubes coming out of me.

Father Paul came back about the same time that a doctor and several other younger looking doctors entered the room. He introduced himself as the orthopedic attending on duty making rounds. He looked at my chart, and started to read off a list of procedures and X-rays that I had had taken to the group of students with him. He asked Father Paul to leave the room so that I could be examined, and I said that I would prefer it if he stayed. The doctor shrugged, and proceeded to undo my hospital gown behind my neck, and flipped it back to show my right shoulder. Father Paul jumped up pulled the sheet up to cover my chest saying, "She's a very modest woman, please respect that as much as you can." The doctor seemed to look at Father Paul's collar, and then nodded his head saying, "Sorry, Father, we get into a hurry sometimes and forget things." He turned to his students and told them to remember their patient's feelings as much as possible.

He raised my arm up and seemed to be testing the range of motion. He asked me to move it around as much as I could without dislodging my IV. He seemed satisfied. He then went around to the left side of bed, pulled the blanket up to expose my left knee. Having both my feet exposed was making me cold. My feet had always been cold ever since my childhood brush with frostbite. He said, "I see you've had some previous knee surgery. What did you have done?" I explained about the torn cartilage. He responded to his students that I had the old style surgery, and that torn cartilage was handled much differently now. He began to move my knee around. "There seems to be some looseness in the joint. I really don't want to just open it up again. You've got a lot of scarring from the previous injury and surgery. Let's try rehab first. Now, I understand you also have a back injury."

He asked me to roll over. This time I was able to roll myself on my left side without assistance, but the pain was indescribable. Every place the doctor touched hurt like a stab. When he allowed me to lie back again, he commented to his students, "It appears to be some pretty substantial tearing of the structure along here." At that he pointed to his own back to demonstrate. "Can anyone tell me which muscles and tendons are probably affected?" Several of the students raised their hands, and repeated a list of Latin sounding names, none of which made any sense to me. Finally, he asked for suggested courses of treatment. None of the students raised their hands.

He turned to me and said, "You have a torque injury to your lower back. The bruising and pain is caused by the stretching or tearing of the muscles and tendons. You haven't gotten any broken bones, but you may have done some damage to the discs between your vertebras. We could do surgery to find out exactly what is going on, but I'd prefer to wait first. Sometimes that kind of back surgery can do more harm than good. Why don't we wait and see first how you recover. You're young and healthy. I don't want to start cutting on you if I don't have to. It's a good sign that you can roll over by yourself now. You couldn't do that yesterday according to your chart. I will be back tomorrow. In the meantime, try to wiggle now and then. We don't want you to stiffen up too much."

After they left the room, Father Paul pulled the blanket back down over my legs, and retied my gown. He looked like he didn't know what to say. Then all of a sudden he said, "I forgot. I've got to go call someone to walk my dog. I'll be right back," and he left the room. When he returned to the room a few minutes later he said, "I will have to leave in about an hour. I have to prepare my homily for mass tonight and tomorrow." That's when I realized that it was already Saturday. What had happened to Friday? Having gaps in my memory was going to be my constant companion for the rest of my life. I was getting the first taste.

Chapter 44: The Mirror Cracked

I became upset that I had missed my class. Fr. Paul laughed that he was pretty sure they would let me make it up. He reminded me that's what the Archbishop had told me when he had been in to visit yesterday. He said if I had trouble, to get the Archbishop to call the professor. I didn't remember his visit at all. Fr. Paul handed me a small icon off the bed side table that he had left for me. The Archbishop and I often had lunch together at the Pastoral Center when I had meetings there. He may have been one of the most holy men I will ever know in my life.

All of a sudden I started crying uncontrollably for no apparent reason. It was something that was going to repeat itself many times over the coming months. He sat on the bed uncomfortably, and cradled my head on his shoulder. He started crying too, and said, "I'm just so sorry this happened to you. I wish I could make it go away. Are you sure that you wouldn't rather have your mom here?" I said, "No, please don't call her." He replied, "I'd feel better leaving if you'd let me call someone to sit with you. How about your Godmother." After I had calmed down, I did ask him to call my next door neighbor. I knew I had left enough food and water out for my dog to last him a couple of days, but I wanted her to check on him. He said he'd do that on his way out.

He sat back in his chair, and obviously was trying to get up the courage to say something. Finally he said, "I know that you don't have a very good relationship with your mother, but you can't go through this all on your own. You don't have to be that independent. Learning to ask for help is good for our souls." Those words would come back to me years later. As he collected his things to leave, he blessed me, kissed my forehead, and held my hand for a moment. He left the room without saying anything else.

Not long after Father Paul left, Dan returned to ask me to look at some photographs. None of them meant anything to me. He said they were people in the neighborhood surrounding my office with criminal records. He asked if I could think of anyone that might want to hurt me. He asked about disgruntled clients. The only two people I could think of at the time were my former boyfriend, Ken, and the members of the Posse that might have wanted to retaliate. Dan was surprised to learn I had testified against a group of white supremacists. He said that he thought if it had been them, I'd be dead. He said, "Great, I guess that means that I'll have to inform the feds." He decided he wanted to check on the alibi of my ex first. When I told him that he worked at a shutter manufacturing company, that especially got his attention. "Cath, you do know that you were stabbed with a wood carving tool. It could be the kind of thing that they would use making wooden shutters. The attack was also on Valentine's Day. I'm starting to think that isn't a coincidence." After getting Ken's information from me, he quickly left the room.

    A couple of hours later another man entered the room. I also recognized him. It was one of the federal agents. I guess he had found out somehow about the attack. He pulled up the chair very close to the bed. "I heard that you had been hurt. I wanted to come by and check on you, and tell you how sorry I am that you have been hurt. I understand from the Chief of Detectives that this might have been an interrupted sexual assault." I told him in confidence that the lead detective was a friend of mine, and put that down so that my name could stay out of the paper. He said, "That was probably smart. I'm actually here to ask you if you remember anything more about the assault. If it is possible that Davidson's men were involved, we are going to want to prosecute this federally."

    I told him I couldn't remember what happened, but I would continue to try to remember, and if anything came up that I felt like could be a help to his investigation, I would call him. I felt that in the meantime, the most important thing was to go about my business as if nothing had happened. He handed me his card, and left the room. It seemed like people had trouble knowing what to say to me. He couldn't seem to take his eye off the cut above my right eye.

    Late that afternoon, my personal physician made an appearance. It had taken them a while to notify her. Actually I think they probably called her for some kind of information. She came in the room, and put her purse down on the bed table. She had picked up my chart on her way in and was looking at it while talking to me. "Hey kiddo, trying to do a Humpty Dumpty imitation I understand?" I told her she didn't need to bother coming if she was going to give me headaches. She replied, "I think you've had enough headaches for one fiscal year." She hit the bed lift, and the head of the bed started going up. "I'm going to just double check some stuff, okay?"

She proceeded to look me all over, and poke and prod on me. I was starting to get sore from how many times I'd been poked on. I normally didn't even like being touched this much. She made me lean forward to look at my back rather than rolling me over. That hurt almost as much. Her only comment was, "Why haven't you been asking for pain killers?" I reminded her that I hated taking any kind of pain medication. "I understand that, but this has really got to hurt. We're going to have to put you on something to get you moving. When you injure your back like this, if you stay down more than a couple of days, it actually hurts more than it helps. We need to get you up today, and it's going to hurt."

"I don't care about it hurting right now. Robin, I'm having trouble remembering what happened. I can't even remember what happened yesterday. I can't seem to keep track of time, and some of the things that the neurologist asked me to do, I couldn't." She sighed heavily, "Do you remember the neurologist talking to you yesterday?" I told her I didn't. "From the notes he put in your file, he believes you have suffered a Traumatic Brain Injury or an Acquired Brain Injury, maybe a bit of both. When someone comes in with a skull fracture or a brain bleed and has to have surgery, we would expect them to have deficits. You've had the kind of injury that we just can't tell immediately if it is the bruising to the brain, or something else. It may all go away, or it may not. It wasn't just the impact to your brain. You were also strangled. We don't know how long the blood flow to your brain may have been cut off. Lack of oxygen can also cause damage that we can't see with any kind of test. I know you don't want to hear this, but it may take some time for us know how extensive the damage is, or how permanent."

I took my glasses off for a minute. I was having trouble seeing through them. There was a large scratch on the right lens where he had originally attempted to stab me in the eye. I started to rub the stitches above my right eye. She said, "Don't do that," and slapped my hand away gently. Then she cocked her head, and said, "Let me look at your eyes again." This time she shined a light in my eyes. "How does your eyesight seem to you? It looks like you've got some redness in them." I told her I was having some trouble being able to read, but thought it was just the concussion. "I think you should have your prescription checked after you go home, it may have changed, but I'd wait at least a month so it can stabilize first."

She picked up my chart, and flipped several pages before finding the one she wanted. She sighed heavily after reading for a few minutes, and muttered to herself, "I'd forgotten about that." I asked her what she was talking about. "The redness in your eyes is called petechial hemorrhages. They can be caused by strangulation, but should pass in a couple of days. Have you been able to eat okay?" I told her that I had only had some broth and some jello. "I'm going to see if you can handle swallowing something more substantial, okay? It's possible that you may have trouble eating solid food for some time to come. You might also have trouble with hoarseness and coughing for awhile. I can order up a throat spray that will help with that."

I had to ask her if there was going to be any permanent damage to my voice. She answered, "I'm not sure right now. Your voice seems fine, but it does seem softer. I wouldn't raise your voice for awhile either. Considering that you're a singer, I'm probably going to want an ear, nose and throat specialist to have a look at it once the swelling goes down. Just take it easy on it for now. Cath, I don't think I need to tell you that you're lucky to be alive. Let's be grateful for that, and worry about your voice later."

She ordered up some medication, and instructed them to get me out of bed as soon as I could tolerate it. She said the quicker I got up, the quicker I could get out of there, and she knew how much I hated hospitals. She wanted me to especially watch for any dizziness when walking. "The last thing we need is for you to fall and hit your head again." So up I went about an hour later. My knee was in a brace, and it didn't hurt as much as I thought it would. My back did. As I rested with the crutches, it almost felt as if my lower half wasn't attached to my top half. It gave me the strange sensation that my body was only being held together by my skin. As long as I could get up and around, I just knew that I would be okay. The walking seemed to be causing a headache, and my ears started ringing. It was a bit like going deep underwater.

Chapter 45: Putting on Masks

I finally went home in a few days on crutches. I had trouble with my knee fairly often, so no one at work thought anything about it when I showed up on them again the following week. My greatest desire was to pretend like nothing had happened. My roommate had returned from her trip to find me in need of a nursemaid. She drove me to work and parked on the other side of the building where there was an elevator. I entered my office from the back door. I know now that I was avoiding the front stairs. Three days after I had been back at work, a woman who worked downstairs on the other side of the building, came up to me in the cafeteria in the basement where I was eating alone. She sat down, and asked me how I was feeling. I didn't really recognize her. I knew she worked in the Lung Association office, but did not know her name.

She could tell I was confused. She introduced herself, and explained that she was the woman who had called 911 after the cleaning woman came into her office screaming. She said she had been the one who told me not to move that help was on the way. She wasn't surprised I didn't remember her. What surprised her is that no one in my office knew I had been hurt. She went in on Friday to ask the receptionist about me, and was told you were going to be out of the office visiting clients in rural areas until the end of the month. When she realized that I had not told them, she didn't press the point. She thought that I must have had my reasons. I thanked her for helping me. She obviously looked like she wanted an explanation but was too polite ask.

I have always been a very private person. I think I grew up feeling like I had to hide myself. Illnesses and injuries were viewed as weaknesses in my stiff back-bone family. With friends, they know everything about me. I often say that the only person I gossip about is myself, but not with strangers. I guess that is when I realized that I didn't consider any of the people I worked with close enough to confide in. This complete stranger knew more about the most important event in my life than the people I had been working along side for years.

I thanked the woman for helping me. I felt the need to explain to her why I hadn't told anyone that I'd been hurt. I admitted to her, and myself at the same time, that I hated the idea of feeling vulnerable. I didn't want to admit that I had been hurt. I didn't want anyone to feel sorry for me, or make a fuss over me. I had shown up at work many times on crutches after hobbling myself with pick up basketball, or sliding into second base playing church league softball. The excuse I used for the bandage on my hand and forehead was a rock climbing accident. That was accepted without question because I had come in with many bruises and abrasions in the past after spending a weekend in Red Rock Canyon.

This woman worked at the Lung Association. She seemed shocked that I had come back to work so quickly, and that I didn't want anyone to know. She said that the police had come to question her about whether she had seen anything. She hadn't. She told me that when the cleaning woman had come to get her, and she saw me sprawled across the bottom two stairs, that she was certain I was dead. She checked my pulse and realized that I was alive, and ran back to call 911. When she came back from making the call, she said I had started to regain consciousness slightly, and that I started praying. She said all she could do was hold my hand and keep me still until the ambulance arrived.

When the EMT's got there, she let them in through the locked front door, and gave them what information she could, which wasn't much. She said as they drove away, she wondered if I was going to make it or not, and the next thing she knows, she sees me in the cafeteria. She and I started having lunch almost everyday together. I think she felt responsible for me, and I felt at ease with her because she knew my big secret. She was the first one to notice that I was having trouble. She caught me accidentally going into the men's room at the end of the hall. I tried to laugh it off, but she could tell it had upset me. All of a sudden I started crying.

In the following months, there were little things that began to crop up. I'd get lost driving to some place that was very familiar. I accidentally ended up in a broom closet in the courthouse. I started missing appointments, losing important documents, and a month later when I sat down to do my taxes, I couldn't understand the forms. I had been doing taxes since I was 12 years old, had taken tax law in law school, was a nationally recognized expert in the tax laws around debt restructuring, and suddenly, I couldn't do my own. I went to my doctor's office without even calling. She worked me in when she saw how agitated I was. I told her about the problems I had been having. She said I had gone back to work too quickly. I told her it was more than that. She sent me downstairs to a lab where a grad student gave me an IQ test. I had taken many over the years. This test showed a 20 point drop.

Chapter 46: Treading Water

To be honest, I remember very little of the next several months. I seemed to be running completely on auto pilot. I took on no new projects. I just tried to do the best I could to manage with what I already had on my plate. Things started to fall away one by one. I withdrew from the Archdiocesan Choir. I had trouble making it to practices, and trouble with my vocal timbre. The ringing in my ear had continued off and on. I eventually even dropped out of the choir at my new parish.

My memory seemed to be getting worse not better with each passing month. In the fall, I found myself unable to keep up with my class, and withdrew. It was just too hard for me. I scheduled no court cases. I would arrange for mediations, but I allowed someone else to handle the actual hearings. I just couldn't do them anymore. It wasn't just that I couldn't seem to understand the issues involved, I was starting to experience panic attacks even thinking about conducting a mediation hearing. There was something about being confronted with the strong emotions or anger that can come out during mediations, that terrified me.

I seemed to be increasingly confused. I would get lost in the grocery store. I would misplace things, forget phone numbers, and become agitated at the least of things. My doctor wanted to try to get me into some kind of rehab program, but my insurance wouldn't pay for it. It was beyond my means as well. All the extra income I used to generate had dried up. I didn't have the energy to work my regular hours. There was none left over to work early or late with private clients. When I think of all the money I wasted on clothing, I'm humiliated. It could easily have paid for the rehabilitation she thought would help me.

Six months after my attack, Dan came to see me. He wanted to know if I could remember anything further about the attack. They had thoroughly gone over Ken's alibi, and couldn't shake it. I still remembered nothing from that day or night. He told me they would have to close the case. Even if I began to remember things, I couldn't testify in court to it. My mental capacity would be called into question. Deep down I knew he was right, but it was so hard for me to accept. No one would ever have to be called to account for the damage done to me. That's when I realized that the date for my Grand Jury testimony had also come and gone without my being called to testify. I guess the feds didn't think I could help them anymore either.

When I went to my doctor shortly after that, she agreed with Dan. She was concerned that even facing someone in court might be too much for me. She was also concerned that I had gained over 25 pounds. She wanted to know if I had changed my diet. I hadn't, but I also wasn't exercising like I had been. She said we'd have to keep an eye on that. The physical injuries seemed to have healed with just a few more scars added to my already scarred body. The scar above my right eye seemed to be well camouflaged by my eyebrow, and the scar on my palm seemed to blend into my life line.

She kind of cocked her head and looked at me for a minute. She looked down at my feet, and then picked up my chart, and flipped to the front. She motioned for me to get back up on the scale, and then pulled the height measurement rod up. After she slid it down to rest on the top of my head, she looked back at my chart again. "Catherine, how tall are you?" I reminded her that I was 5'10". We had joked once that I was the shortest you could be and belong to the tall people's club. She double checked the rod again, and said, "It looks like you've lost some height, maybe as much as an inch." At that news, I felt like I slumped even shorter.

She did some testing on my left hand for strength and dexterity, and was really surprised. She wanted to know if I had been playing any guitar at all since the injury. I told her I hadn't been able to pick any instrument up. It was as if my hand just wouldn't follow commands anymore. It wasn't just my left hand, I had trouble remembering the chords, let alone forcing my hand to make them. I had played since I was child when a neighbor had given me an old guitar. I bought a book, and just started playing. There were times when I made tuition money playing in a band. I wrote my first song at

14. I always felt such elation playing, especially in church. It had been such an outlet for me in my life, and that seemed to now be in the past.

It was as if the stress of the injuries had also left me unable to engage in the very activities I would normally have used to deal with the stress. I could no longer engage in sports, play music, or even just have a quiet time. My life was no longer quiet. I had constant noise in my ears, and sometimes, this white noise became something different. Sometimes I thought I heard screaming. I thought I was beginning to lose my mind.

Chapter 47: Last Call

At one time I could prepare my entire case in my head before appearing in court. I knew every participant and I memorized every question I wanted to ask. I took pride in that. Now my brain would not retain the information. I began to organize the witnesses on index cards. One side would be an outline of who the witness was and what they had said in their depositions. The other side was for questions I wanted to ask. That seemed to be working well for me in the beginning. That is until I accidentally dropped the cards in the middle of a trial. It was obvious to everyone in the courtroom that I did not know what I was going to do. The judge called a recess for me to compose myself. It was an important case to me. It ended up being my last court room appearance. I was representing a friend from church. She was trying to get custody of her granddaughter. Her son had died of AIDS, and the girl's mother had been living with a pedophile. We ended up winning the case after I put my cards back in the proper order.

I had never lost a case that I contested. I was called the next day by someone I worked with occasionally at the Department of Corrections. He was head of the victim/offender mediation program, and we had originally taken mediation certification together. He also had a position with the Bar Association. He wanted to take me to lunch. I thought that he had heard about my injuries somehow, and wanted to give condolences. I had been receiving many of those types of calls in the time since being injured as the story began to be commonly known. I just thought I could keep it a secret. He made it clear that he was there representing the Bar. He said the judge in my last case had made a call to the Bar about my competency.

He seemed embarrassed to tell me that he did not want me to face a competency hearing. He got permission to talk to me instead. If I would agree to refrain from trying court cases, they would allow me to keep my license. He recommended that I medically retire. He said, "Cath, you have always given your best to your clients, and you can't do that anymore. I've had to have these conversations with attorneys who have had strokes or heart attacks. It's never easy. Please don't let them publicly humiliate you."

I thanked him for his honesty. This was one person whose opinion I actually listened to. I knew he was right. He added something else before he left, "I heard about your testimony. I wanted to thank you. Not many white people would be willing to stand up like that." As he walked away, I realized that he was African-American. I never thought about him that way until that moment. He was what the Colonel would have called a mud person.

I walked down the street, and walked into the bar where I had celebrated my first court victory. At that time of day, it was mostly empty. I sat at the bar, and got more intoxicated that I had been since college. I had to call my roommate to come drive me home. That was how it ended, with a whimper. I would never again enter a regular court room. I was the first person in my graduating class to be published in the Bar Journal, first to become an ATLA member, the first to win a court case, and now the first to retire from the court room.

I started catching flashes of images before my eyes. Sometimes it was like seeing a hand coming towards my face. I would startle, duck or cower only to discover that nothing was coming at me. I began to startle when someone dropped something on the tile floor. The phone especially began to bother me. I found it increasingly difficult to make phone calls. My heart would begin to race, and I would break out in a cold sweat. The sound of the phone ringing would wake me from a sound sleep. I thought someone was trying to harass me, so I started turning off the ringer before going to bed. The ringing continued. Even with the phone unplugged, the sound of a ringing phone would wake me up repeatedly. I had to finally accept the fact that the ringing I was hearing wasn't coming from my phone, but from my head.

That fall we had a problem with the office. While workers were repairing the roof, it began to rain. Water poured through the building. What was worse, when they came back to finish to job, they didn't repair the water damage, they just covered it over. Everyone in the building began to suffer respiratory problems.

Eventually the roofer's insurance company came in to attempt to clean the building up. Overnight they cleaned the duct work with a solvent that leaked onto our tile floor. By the time we started the day, it had dried very slippery. I fell. My knee was again injured.

This time I received some serious rehab, but eventually I had to agree to more surgery. It was just supposed to be outpatient surgery. I was going to get to go home that night, but something went wrong. I have been in recovery rooms many times. That first awakening after anesthesia is disconcerting, but this time felt different. I couldn't seem to wake up, and I started vomiting. I still do not know if I was given too much anesthetic, or if it was my brain injury affecting the level I needed. I had to stay in the hospital over night for observation.

I did get to see a video of the inside of my knee that was gross and surreal. The doctor vacuumed out what was left of my ACL. He also resurfaced the edges. In the 11 years since my previous knee surgery, I had developed arthritis in the joint. There are a lot of former athletes running around with arthritis in their knees and are having to have the joint replaced because they had the old surgery like I did. They officially diagnosed the arthritis in my knee on my 30th birthday. It was a great birthday present.

Our contract with the State Department of Agriculture had grown every year, with the additional money that the federal government began paying in matching grants; we finally had some breathing room. What it also caused unfortunately was interest by other organizations in getting a piece of the pie. The Ag Department was forced to open the contract up to bidding. In the past I had always prepared all the reports necessary for the contract. I found myself unable to prepare them just when it was most important.

As part of the yearly administrative issues, the new director, a Methodist minister, decided to do performance reviews. When he brought me in, he became very paternal towards me. He had noticed the marked downturn in both the quantity and quality of my work. He said that when I was in the office, I did the work of 4 people, but I was missing more and more office hours. Then he hit me with a stunner. He thought I had a developed some kind of chemical dependence. He had just come back from a chemical dependency workshop and was seeing alcoholics under every rock. I had to laugh out loud. When I missed work it was usually because I was in too much pain to move because I refused to take even the mild pain killer the doctor prescribed. To be honest, I don't remember how the rest of that interview went, so I don't know how I convinced him that I wasn't an alcoholic.

Chapter 48: Descent

I was still walking with a cane after my knee surgery when we got the news that we had lost the Ag Department contract. I felt responsible for 8 people losing their jobs including 3 single moms, and oh yeah, me too. I began packing my law books and files into boxes. The few open cases I had, I turned over to Legal Aid. As I started to go downstairs with the files, I stopped at the top of the stairs and looked around. They really were quite pretty, Sweeping, curving, cream colored marble looking out over two stories of glass. I turned and looked at an impression in the wall next to my office door made during our struggle. I ran my hand across it. It would be the only witness left to tell the tale.

I hated goodbyes. I wrote a great letter of recommendation for my secretary, loaded the boxes up in my car, and left the parking lot one last time. I went down to file for unemployment the next day for the first time in my life. Because of my recent knee surgery, they made me get a letter from my doctor that I was released to return to work. I went off to my regular doctor. Robin gave me a very thorough going over, including an extensive test of my coordination and mental acuity.

I flunked. She said in good conscience that she couldn't recommend that I return to work. She would be more than happy to file disability forms for me, but she was afraid that the stress of a full time job was just too much for me. She was afraid that I would have an accident and get hurt even worse. She said, "Cath, you aren't the same person now that you were before the attack. You are probably never going to be that person again. Every time you come into this office, you are more stooped over to the right, you seem more confused, and I'm concerned that you aren't sleeping properly. You were hurt really badly. There's no shame in admitting that you are disabled. How many disabled people have you helped over the years. They were all at the place you are now. Let me help you."

I left her office with the forms I needed to file for disability and some brochures on support groups for brain injury survivors. I deposited both in the trash can at the door downstairs. I made an appointment with the doctor who did my knee surgery. I got him to sign the paperwork for unemployment. All he was concerned with is that my knee surgery had healed. I spent 12 months on unemployment. That was the maximum time allowed then. I had thought about trying to open my own law office, but I knew that I would not be able to successfully run one. I doubted that I would be able to keep all the paperwork straight. In the time I was on unemployment, I applied for over 100 state jobs. I took every merit test that I was remotely qualified for. I have always worked. I believed in work as part of my self worth.

  The state of Oklahoma had a merit based system. Those who made the top 5 grades on any given test for a specific job had to be given an interview. They didn't have to be hired, but they had to be given a chance. With no job stresses other than trying to find a job, I actually did well on the tests. I was ranked #1 on every merit test I took. I took tests for forestry and parks jobs, for child support enforcement, secretarial, you name it. I even applied for a job doing landscaping work at a horse farm.

  In that year, I got two interviews, only one through the merit system. That job was in the mail room of the state capital. Coming to an interview for a job that required lifting heavy mail sacks while still walking with a cane, was not what they wanted in a new worker. The fact that I was a tad over qualified probably didn't help. The other interview I got was in Dallas with a non-profit law firm that worked with the disabled. I got to the second interview with that agency, and it became apparent that I couldn't follow some of the questions they were trying to ask me. Their first interview had been over the phone. The second interview had been in Dallas. The 3 hour drive had been so tiring, that by the time I got there, I was wasted.

  They were very nice to me. They spent all their time representing clients with disabilities. They knew one when they saw one. Half way through the interview, the Executive Director called a break to speak to me in private. She had been a nurse before going to law school. She questioned me about my injuries. She said that I seemed to be listing to the right, and kept turning my head as if I was having trouble hearing out of one of my ears. I actually felt relieved to tell her that my doctor didn't want me working. She thanked me for being so honest with her. She asked me how I would feel if I hired someone who was trying to work through serious disabilities while on the job before they were ready, and they re-injured themselves or worse.

I withdrew my application for the position, but thanked her for considering me. She asked me if I remembered her. I had to admit that I didn't recognize her. She had been in a continuing legal education class I had taught several years ago. She said she hadn't heard that I had been hurt until she called on some of the references listed on my application. She was so sorry. She even offered to have her agency help with my disability paperwork. She did make me wonder what people were saying about me, but she wouldn't tell me because of confidentiality.

I drove home from Dallas, and it was the scariest drive of my life. It is a straight shot up I-35. I have driven it hundreds of times, but this time, I got lost somehow. I got really lost. I did the only thing I knew to do. I pulled into the next motel parking lot, and got a room for the night. I thought a good night's sleep would make everything okay in the morning. The problem was that I didn't get a good night's sleep. I began to have horrible night mares. The stress of being unemployed, the trip to Dallas, the feeling that someone who had respected me now pitied me, and the overwhelming fear of getting lost, had broken me.

I spent two days at that motel. I seemed to be remembering the attack in my dreams only to have it just outside my reach when waking. I could remember sounds, smells, and flashes of disconnected scenes. I still didn't know who had hurt me, but I knew I was starting to remember. Unfortunately the few things I did remember seemed to be invading my every thought. When I was finally able to straighten myself enough to find my way home, I went straight to the doctor's office.

Chapter 49: Accepting the Inevitable

I had been surviving on very little sleep for months. Eventually I started dreaming about the attack. Since I had no real memory of the attack previously, I could almost tell myself it hadn't happened. The first memories had been physical. I would feel a jolt and relive the pain of one of my stab wounds. It was as if I could feel the steel going into my hand like it was happening again. I caught myself rubbing my hand constantly. I also would hear a horrible cracking sound in my head and start shaking. I guess it must have been the sound my head made when it hit the marble.

I found myself nervous just sitting in the waiting room. I felt like I was going to start crying. I actually started to have trouble breathing. I think the nurse noticed that I was having some kind of anxiety attack. She took me to an exam room in the back, and let me keep the door open. When Robin finally came in the room, her first comment was, "God you look like hell. I almost didn't recognize you. What's going on?" I didn't want to tell her. I thought she would put me in a mental hospital, but I was too afraid not to tell her. When I told her about the trip to Dallas, the confusion, the nightmares, the memories invading everything, she said, "Kiddo, what you're describing is called Post Traumatic Stress Disorder." I looked at her in shock and said, "That's what war veterans get. I can't have that."

She walked across the room. I felt another brochure coming on. Instead she brought a sample package of medication to hand me. "This medicine is showing some success in treating PTSD, but there are no guarantees. Let's try it for a few months and see if it helps any. Now how are you feeling otherwise? You look like you've gained some more weight too. Are you eating any differently?" I replied, "I haven't really thought about it, but my clothes are getting pretty tight. Maybe I'm just spending too much time at home."

Robin went over and got out a sheet to have me take some blood work. That's when I had to tell her that I had lost my health insurance when I lost my job, and couldn't afford several hundred dollars for extensive blood work. She put her hand to her forehead, and said,

"Cath, you're going to have to find some way to get this blood work done. It's important. Not many people survive as serious a strangling as you had. You could have some damage to your thyroid. It's in that part of your neck. If you would agree to go on disability, you could get back on insurance."

I got angry, angrier than I had been in a long time. I yelled at her that I was an important attorney, and that I didn't need anyone telling me that I couldn't practice anymore. She asked me how long it had been since I had been in court, and I told her over 6 months. She said, "You were an important attorney, once. Now you are a woman who is really hurt, and hurting. You've help so many people over the years, why won't you let anyone help you now?" I said, "Fine, if everyone thinks that I am such a reject, I will apply for my pension, but they won't give it to me. I did enough of these applications to know that they are all turned down the first time. I'm an attorney. There are attorneys who are quadriplegic. I'm not that handicapped." "Cath, quadriplegics are just paralyzed. They can still use their minds. Your brain has been hurt. It just won't let you work the way you used to."

I agreed to submit the paperwork, and much to my surprise, my pension was approved in 3 months flat, and they even gave me a lump sum going back to the last day I worked at the Council, even though I had drawn unemployment for a year. My full insurance wouldn't start for another year. In the meantime, my doctor saw me for free. I had always done her taxes for free, so it seemed only fair. Everything else, I had to go to the medical school for.

I started to have one strange medical problem after another. First, my stomach started giving me fits again. Eventually my doctor ordered up an endoscope of my stomach. She thought I had developed an ulcer. The pictures that came back showed the entire lining of my stomach was seriously inflamed. She said acute stress syndrome can cause my body to produce too much acid. There was a medicine for it, an expensive medicine.

Next I woke up one morning and literally did not know which end was up. My roommate had to call an ambulance. They strapped me on a gurney because I was convinced I was going to fall off, up. The diagnosis was labyrinthitis. It's a severe form of vertigo, and common among those who have had head injuries. They put me on a table, tilted my head down, and took X-rays straight up my nose. It was bizarre, and a pretty cruel thing to do to someone who doesn't know which way is up. The PTSD medication seemed to be helping with the nightmares and panic attacks, but I started to really gain weight.

Curveballs

Chapter 50: Who is That in the Mirror

I have never been what high fashion would call svelte. I have always been a large woman. As a child, I was like a St. Bernard puppy that everyone just knew was going to be a big dog. I think I grew into my father's shoes about the age of 9. I was an athlete, but I tended to gain weight every time I stopped playing either for summer vacation or an injury rehab. What was happening now though, was beyond belief. Within a year of going on the medication, I gained 100 pounds. I'd like to be able to blame the medicine for all of it, but I'm not going to do that. I am ultimately responsible for everything that went into my mouth.

The lost of my job, my career, obviously caused depression. I did not ask for help easily. I still don't. I think I ate more because of the depression, and I also seemed to eating to sedate myself in a way. When I was eating, the flashbacks were much less severe. It was as if everything in my old life was being peeled away one layer at a time. As I gained weight, my extensive wardrobe was no longer of any use to me. That Lent saw me giving it all up. A nun I worked with occasionally at Catholic Charities was the recipient.

My pension obviously didn't pay as much as my former occupation had. I lost my home, my clothes, my career, and the feeling of security that comes from "things". I truthfully do not miss those things now. I am embarrassed by the materialistic, arrogant person I once was. I vowed to never be that person again. I began volunteering my time again helping other disabled people file for their pensions. This time, I didn't keep the 20% lawyers fees. I may have agreed to go on disability, but I kept my license to practice law. As long as I didn't over extend myself, I seemed to be able to manage. I would only take one client at a time.

I spent every Wednesday morning at the Social Security offices in the Murrah Federal Building. I would sometimes run into one of the federal agents I had worked with in the lobby. They always were very cordial, and asked how I was doing. They never asked if my memory was returning. I guess at that point it wouldn't have mattered. They used to joke that they knew I was in the building when they saw my car in my "assigned" space. The Murrah building had ample handicap parking on the South side of the building. It was just a long walk from there to the Social Security offices on the North side of the building. There was one lone handicap parking space in front of the loading zone on the North side of the building that was rarely used because that side of the building had steps. I walked with a cane, but could still navigate steps.

By this time, my roommate had regained custody of her oldest son. I found myself raising a child. She wasn't capable of taking care of him by herself, and I wasn't willing to allow another child to enter the foster care system. He was a chemical exposure baby who had so many socialization problems that I was afraid of how he would cope in foster care. I also believed at the time that I was too damaged for any man to want me as his wife, so I guess I created the family I knew I would never have.

That's what I did for the first two years after losing my job. I puttered. I volunteered, I mothered, and I continued to take my theology classes at night. With the slower pace of my life, I was able to go back to school, but my grades were never as good after my injuries as they had been before. I also found it painful to sit in class for 3 hours, and often had to leave before class was over. I was still unwilling to just throw medication at the problem. Besides, the amount of medicine it would have taken to allow me to sit on a hard chair for 3 hours would have made me not capable of safely driving home after class.

I took up old hobbies to keep myself occupied. I began to sew again. I originally did so because with kids, something always needs mending. I started sewing new clothes for myself, but no silk dresses. I eventually began to sew things for church like banners and liturgical vestments. My mother had done a lot of that over the years. I found that these things came back to me so easily. I could remember how to alter a pattern, or do a French seam. Things I had learned years before, but I still couldn't remember enough Spanish to even say hello. I did find I could still read it. My doctor found that fascinating. She decided that my brain must have been damaged where I stored spoken Spanish and French, but not where I stored the written parts.

As the third anniversary of my attack approached, I began to get the feeling that I was being followed again. I especially noticed it on Wednesdays after leaving the Social Security office. I still to this day can not remember the face of the man who attacked me, and at that time, I still did not know if I had been attacked by my ex-boyfriend, a neo-Nazi, or just some stranger. The realization that it was probably because of my testimony was really hard for me to accept. I think I wanted it to be anything else but that because that was the scariest option.

As I was coming out of the federal building one afternoon, I thought I saw a familiar truck parked in the lot across the street to the North of the entrance. As I was standing there looking across the street, that first female agent I had worked with walked past me into the building. She casually waved. It's as if, an important epiphany hit me. If someone from the farm had been responsible for my attack, and they were following me again, then they would have seen me go into the same building every week that I had originally gone into when I was preparing for my testimony against them.

I walked very quickly back inside the building, and caught up to the agent. I pulled her to one side, and asked her if anything was going on with Davidson's case. She said she wasn't at liberty to discuss things like that in an open investigation. That's all I needed to hear. The investigation was still open, and I was being seen going into their building every week. I realized that I might be in danger again. This time, I had the added fear of being responsible for a small child. I didn't know what to do.

Chapter 51: Finally Fleeing

I did a lot of praying over the next several days. I called Fr. Paul out of the blue and asked him if I could buy him lunch. He seemed delighted to hear from me. Normally he got to see me only twice a year. During Lent and Advent, churches often had large penitential services that priests from all the parishes got together to help with. I would find out which ones he went to, and then be the last in line for his booth. I could go to confession, he could find out how I was doing. I could get a big hug. It wasn't much, but I didn't have to worry about anyone seeing us together. I could even slip him his Christmas presents.

I got to the restaurant first, and when he came in, he walked right past me. He didn't recognize me. I called after him, and he turned around and did a double take. At first he was smiling, and when he sat down and looked at me, he said, "Are you okay? You look awful." I told him that was what every woman wanted to hear. He reached his hand across the table, and patted the pack of my hand. I had forgotten how much I missed getting to see him.

I thought I'd save him the trouble of asking. "Yes, I've gained a lot of weight. I started having PTSD symptoms, and the doctor put me on some medicine that seems to help, but it makes you gain weight. She also thinks I might have gotten my thyroid damaged in the attack. It's in the neck. I never knew that before, and my injuries really keep me from being able to get much exercise." He wanted to know what I had been doing, and I told him. He told me what everyone at church was up to. We had a really great time catching up.

Finally over dessert, he got around to asking me why I had called him out of the blue. He loved seeing me, but I must have something really important to talk to him about. I told him about thinking that I was being followed to the federal building, and that the case against Davidson was still open. I admitted to him finally that I was afraid again. Without hesitation, he said, "You need to leave the state, Catherine. Go some place far away where no one knows you, and don't look back. I'd miss you, but I miss you now. I got used to having you around, but I don't think I could survive seeing you hurt again. It was too hard. I had always wanted to do your wedding, I will not do your funeral." With that, he got up, kissed me on the forehead, whispered I love you in my ear, and left the restaurant.

A week later, we were hit by an ice storm, and there wasn't much else I could do but stay inside. My roommate came home from venturing out on the ice, and exclaimed that she was sick of winters, and we should move some place warmer. I immediately agreed. She was rather shocked. I had not broached the subject of moving to her yet. People raised in Oklahoma tend to have a mindset that we are at the end of the road, and there is no where else to go. We may complain and talk about leaving, but just never do. People that do leave to go into the military or get jobs in Texas are the exception.

The idea of just deciding to move somewhere else, is unheard of, and I hadn't mentioned it to her, because I didn't know if I wanted to take her with me or not. I didn't know if she would want to move away from her younger son. I did know that I couldn't just leave. She still wasn't capable of taking care of her older son by herself. I did feel responsible in that regard. I think I also knew deep down that it wasn't good for me to live alone. There were days that I had a harder time with my injuries. It was good for me to know that if I got confused or lost, or if my other injuries acted up, that I had someone I could call. She decided she wanted to go with me. Maybe a new place would be good for her too.

Everywhere I went in Oklahoma, someone knew me, had known my dad, or knew some other member of my family. My mother once told me to be careful what I did in public because someone would see it, and it would eventually get back to her. She was right. I could never do anything and get away with it for long before she found out about it. I needed to go somewhere new, a place where no one knew me, or any member of my family. I went to the library and picked out some books on places to retire or move to. I set up criteria as if I was doing a research project. I eventually settled on St. Petersburg, Florida, a place I had never been to, and didn't even know anyone who had been there or lived there.

To finance the move, I sold most of my accumulated possessions. I no longer felt the need for possessions. I didn't need antique furniture or art work anymore. I sold the bicycle that my brother John had given me when I went away to college. It was a Motobecane GT. It had originally been blue, but he painted it yellow for me. He knew I needed the men's model because the women's weren't big enough for me, so he wanted to "soften" it a bit for me. I loved that bike, I had put hundreds of miles on it, but I was no longer able to ride. I was just glad it went to someone I knew. One of my college friends bought it for her daughter. I walked away from my bike and all my climbing equipment. I even sold my chain saw.

The hardest sales were my musical instruments. Each one had been lovingly chosen and treasured. The first to find a new home was my Fender Stratocaster. I had originally bought it for my nephew. I thought he might find it something to do rather than get high. I was primarily an acoustic guitar person, but that was sweet ax. I never played it in public, but when I was in the right mood, everyone on the block could hear it.

I also quickly sold my banjo. I had bought it for myself for Christmas right before I got hurt. It was Deering 6 string that I had custom made with burl walnut and abalone inlay. It was supposed to be a good banjo for guitar players to learn on. I was going to buy myself some lessons for my birthday a month after my attack. I never even got to have my first lesson on it. I did get a great price for it, as I did for my mandolin. It was a small 100 year old Russian made one. It had such sweet tones. I remember the first time I picked it up I knew I had to play it, and after I played it, I knew I had to have it. I had found it in a flea market years before. I had tried playing it only once after the injury to my hand. I couldn't get my hand to make even the simplest chord on its slender neck.

Of all my instruments, I had my acoustic guitar the longest. My father had taken me down to the pawn shops by the stockyards when I was in junior high school to get it. I had been saving my babysitting money to get a better guitar than the beater that I had learned on. He said a lot of musicians have to pawn their instruments when they run into trouble, and that was the place to get something good, something worth playing on. It was a 1965 dove model. One of the nuns at church who taught me many great techniques on the guitar had one like it. I figured if it was good enough for a nun, it was good enough for me. My dad got the pawnbroker down to $100 including the hard shell case. My dad was always a good negotiator. I would have paid the price on the tag and been ecstatic, but getting it for a better price also gave me a good feeling.

When I close my eyes, I can still see that dove on the pick guard and the little flowers around it, I can smell the honeysuckle on the trees in the garden behind the bar my band used to play at, I can feel that pure joy again of just letting loose with a major solo right in the middle of a song when no one was expecting it, playing so hard that I broke out in a sweat, and broke a string. The memories were all I had left. I couldn't bear the idea of selling it though. I knew I'd probably never be able to play in public again, and it was just a constant reminder of what I had lost. I drove over to the elementary school where the nun who taught me my first real lessons worked at now. She didn't recognize me. I handed it to her, and asked her to give it to one of her students, someone who couldn't afford a nice guitar to learn on; someone who showed a spark of talent. I just wanted it to be loved again.

Chapter 52: Saying Goodbye

My mother was confused as to why I was planning to move to Florida. I'm glad I waited until almost the last minute. I had never told her about my attack. It took me 16 years to finally tell her. She had taken such pleasure in telling people that her daughter was a lawyer. She didn't understand what was going on, and I didn't want to talk about it. I let her come over and look through stuff to see if she wanted anything before it went out to a garage sale. I didn't have much to say, and neither did she.

Other goodbyes were harder. I went to see my Godmother. She also didn't understand, until she saw me. When I got busy with my career, I usually only got to see her on Christmas Eve. Calling her out of the blue didn't faze her though. She could almost sense that something was wrong. I came in and pulled up a chair to her dining table, and looked out the window towards the creek that I had once been snowbound in. I said, "Ralph, I need to leave town. I got hurt. I got hurt really bad. I testified against some bad men, and I think they may have been the ones who hurt me. I think they may want to hurt me again, and I'm scared."

She came over and sat down next to me saying, "I knew there was something wrong last Christmas. You just didn't seem yourself. I thought maybe you were just working too hard. I asked your mother, and she said that you had lost your job. I couldn't imagine that happening, so I knew there was something else going on. Who did you testify against? Did you see someone doing something? If you testified against them, why aren't they in jail?" I explained to her what I had done. She got really quiet, and then said, "Yes, you need to leave, and don't look back. Just be safe."

As I was getting up to leave, she gave me a hug, and said, "I came to see you in court once. I had gone to your office to surprise you for lunch, and your secretary told me where you were. I got there in time to see your closing argument. I was so proud of you. I was so happy that you seemed to have found a way to spend your life helping people. Now you're going to have to find another way. Just remember that everything you do stands witness to who you are, but don't forget to try to be happy too."

When I left her house, I drove to the cemetery where my father is buried. I stopped first at the lullaby land where my infant nephew is buried. I was thinking about the day that my father had come to tell me that Bobby had died. My dad told me that he had gone to the angels. He was buried right next to the duck pond, and I always saved my stale bread to feed them when I came to visit.

Next I drove to the section where I could see the lone tree that my father was buried next to. I pulled some grass that had grown too close to his stone. I knew I would miss being able to visit his grave, but it didn't matter. I take my father with me everywhere I go. I see him every time I look in the mirror. I have his eyes, ears, and nose. I even have his crooked smile and the same small mole just above my lip. His blood flows in my veins. I often wonder if he would have been proud of me, and as soon as I wonder, I know the answer. He was proud of me even when I fell down or sat the bench.

In the last month before we left, I got the opportunity to attend Easter services at my old church. I sat in the back of the over crowded sanctuary, and looked around at all my old friends. No one recognized me. I listened to Fr. Paul give one of his great sermons about new life. Within a few short weeks, Fr. Paul would also be moving on to a new parish. The whole thing felt like going back to visit your old high school, and nothing seeming the same. It did make it a lot easier to say goodbye.

The week before we left, I made another trip over to my old neighborhood. I went to the mall where Oma now worked. She worked in the Junior miss department of a large store. She wasn't there for a change. I took a chance and drove over to her home. There she was, puttering around in the front garden. I thought about telling her why I was moving, but I decided not to. She's a very sensitive and caring person. I didn't want to burden her with it. We sat and talked about her kids, and things at church like we always did. When I left, she gave me a big hug, the kind that would have to last for a long time. She handled it better than I did. Being an Air Force wife, she was used to goodbyes.

That just left himself. I knew I needed to say goodbye to Fr. Paul. I just didn't know how. He used to eat breakfast every morning at the same fast food restaurant up the street from the church. I went in and sat down across from him. I didn't know what to say. Finally, I said that I was leaving in a week for Florida. He said, "Am I to take it that this isn't to go to Disney on vacation." I reminded him that the whole thing was his idea in the first place. He said, "The one time you actually take my advice, and I wish you weren't. Just promise me that you'll take good care of yourself, and keep in touch with me. I'll always be here if you need me."

He had no words of wisdom, no memorable last words. He just finished his breakfast in silence, and I walked back to the rectory with him. I looked over the hedges I had planted three years before, and found them to be doing fine without me. I realized that everyone was going to be fine without me. When we got to the rectory door, he turned to me and said, "I will miss you. Do you need some empty boxes?" He always had a way of making me smile. I passed on the boxes, gave him a hug, and walked away before either of us had the chance to fall apart. I even drove past my old house. It looked the same as the day I left it, except the bushes needed trimming. I did wonder if I would every be back this way again.

With the last loose ends tied up, we loaded up our remaining furniture and clothes into a large u-haul truck, and I began a very long drive. I had the load shift on the high overpass in Dallas, clipped a car parked in a fire zone in Louisiana, and got lost once or twice too. Coming across the Howard Franklin Bridge, and seeing the Pinellas peninsula for the first time, was overwhelming. It was so pretty. It was beautiful in a way that a girl from the red dirt prairies just couldn't conceive of at first. It felt like home the minute we rested our weary feet in the warm sand. I felt something else for the first time in a very long time – safe.

Chapter 53: A Fresh Start

After we got settled, I threw myself into learning new things. I had never really fished, but it seemed to be something that everyone in Florida did. We had fishermen in Oklahoma, just not many fish. My roommate had liked to fish, and was anxious to try her hand at the saltwater kind. I went along to give myself and the dog some fresh air. The first time I wet a line in St. Pete, I caught a 30 lb. sting ray. That will hook you on fishing really quickly. It scared me half to death, so I released it. Eventually, I took up flats fly fishing. I even learned to tie my own flies. I tried so desperately to learn new things. I was afraid of what might happen to me if I let my mind relax. The brain injury terrified me at times. I had seen my grandfather suffer with dementia. That is a ghost that chases me to this day.

We lay on beaches; I learned to snorkel properly. The water is the one place I never felt like a cripple. I started making custom clerical shirts. My main customers turned out to be Protestant female ministers. Apparently the over the counter clerical shirts were designed for men. Go figure. Those women, with more ample busts than the typical Catholic priest has, were kind of stuck. I had one women order 12 all at one time. She was going through menopause, and needed to wear her shirts un-tucked because of hot flashes. Stock clerical shirts are all designed to be tucked. I never made much money off the business, but it was nice to feel needed again for some type of skill.

Less than a year after we moved, I was sitting at the sewing machine, when my roommate yelled at me to come in and look at the TV. The Oklahoma City federal building had blown up. I sat in stunned silence watching it all unfold. In the coming days and weeks, I stayed in front of the TV. I actually used the telephone trying to find out information about the people I worked with in that building. We eventually discovered that Tim McVey parked the rental truck in the loading zone right next to what everyone called my parking space. The people who oversaw our matching federal funds from the US Agriculture Department, the older brother of someone I went to school with, and almost all the people I worked with at the Social Security office, were dead.

The church next door that I used to love going to noon mass at, was nearly destroyed. All the antique stained glass windows were blown to bits. The two agents that had originally interviewed me, in fact all the people involved in my testimony, survived, but not the files involved. Even the tape recordings I had made at rural meetings, and turned over to the government, were destroyed either by the explosion, the fires, or the eventual demolition. Had I stayed in Oklahoma, there is no doubt in my mind that I would have been in the building when it was attacked. I went there every Wednesday morning like clockwork.

When it came out that the bombers were white supremacists, it made me so angry. I just didn't understand the kind of hate these people lived on. Where does it come from? Children are born so loving, adults have to teach them to hate. It was the first time that I saw anything positive from my injuries. Had I not fled the state, I would probably have died in the explosion. God obviously had something else in mind for my life. I just wished that he would let me in on it.

Chapter 54: When You Least Expect It

My life took a drastic change in 1996. We had been in Florida for two years, and were in the process of a move. I picked up a box, turned with it, and went straight to the floor. I had to crawl over to my van and crawl in the back so that my roommate could drive me straight to the hospital. By this time I had gained a substantial amount of weight, and found out quickly that I made doctors uncomfortable. When I was an athlete, doctors would listen to me, and seemed to want to treat me. After gaining a lot of weight, I found the opposite to be true. Doctors sometimes seemed like they were afraid to touch me.

I spent hours in the emergency room. There are a large number of drug addicts in Florida who feign back injuries in order to get prescriptions. I was looked at very critically from the moment I entered the hospital. If they had actually known how much I disliked any kind of pain medication, maybe I would have gotten better treatment. The female doctor in the ER acted as if she thought I was some kind of filth. I received no treatment of any kind. With my medical history, it would have made sense to at least do an X-ray or an MRI on my back. She ordered neither. Every hour or so, she would send in the nurse to release me. I refused to be released until I was examined or treated. I could not sit up, let alone walk out of the ER.

After many hours spent just lying on a gurney shoved in the corner, in agony, unable to move, my roommate went into the waiting room and called my doctor. She was a new doctor because I had just changed HMO's, and I had not even met her yet. My roommate explained what was going on, and my doctor called the ER doctor and insisted that I be examined. Instead, she pumped me full of muscle relaxers, and called two ambulances to take me home since she figured it would take 4 EMT's to get me in and out of the ambulance. I hadn't come to the hospital in an ambulance but went home in one. I spent the next 7 weeks of my life unable to move from bed. It was my roommate's turn to take care of me.

I couldn't get out of bed to be seen by my new doctor. After almost two months, I was able to finally walk about 10 feet on crutches. That meant I could make it from the bedroom to the living room, and then to the drive. My roommate drove me to the doctor's office, and I just made it inside before collapsing. The pain brought back all the pain of my attack. I had re-injured the same muscles, tendons, and discs that were originally damaged. This time it was devastating. I could no longer stand up straight. I could only stand for a few short seconds at a time. My back looked like a corkscrew. I ended up in a wheelchair. In a way, it was liberating. After all those weeks in bed, I could at least get out of the house and into the sunshine again.

I had to learn how to do things all over again. I had been tall since the age of 11. I was used to looking down towards other women, and looking eye to eye with men. Now I was adjusting to living my life sitting down. The biggest adjustment was learning how to roll a wheelchair that was designed to be pushed. I guess manufacturers figure that if you are over a certain size, and you need a wheelchair, that you aren't able to push yourself. The back wheels were set so far back, I could barely reach them. Arm rests on wheelchairs are lower in the front to allow you to slide up under tables. I had to reverse them so that the lower part was towards the back to allow me to reach the wheels easier. That chair took me everywhere I needed to go for the next 8 years.

Chapter 55: Mother Hubbard

I threw myself into being a "soccer" mom. Shortly after we moved to Florida, my roommate was given custody of her youngest son as well. He was now 7 years old, and his older brother was now 10. I threw myself into Boy Scouts and little league. The younger boy had been neglected. He had never been to the dentist, and his diet had consisted of almost entirely sugar. He was also a chemical exposure child. He came to us after just completing 1st grade, and he couldn't read because he had no reason to bother. His step-mother had told him that reading was for chumps. I couldn't in good conscience just send him off to 2nd grade to be behind from the beginning.

I decided to homeschool both boys. It was a wonderful bonding experience. We did that for 2 years. I only put a stop to it when it was apparent that the boys began to like the "home" part better than the "school" part. When they returned to public school, the older boy had placed two grades ahead. I only let them put him up one year. I didn't want him being lost as the smallest kid. He had actually started school a year behind because of developmental delays, so this was putting him back in the grade he should have been originally. The younger boy was caught up, plus some, as well. I constantly had to remind myself that I couldn't treat both boys the same. I had to treat them equally, but they each had their own unique needs.

The older boy was quiet and withdrawn. He could sit in a corner not moving, reading a book for hours. The younger child never sat down. We had to find something for each to do at their own level. The oldest found Boy Scouts to be a good fit, and eventually made Eagle Scout. The youngest played baseball. I mean he literally played baseball every waking moment. In Florida, that is a year around sport, and he played on two teams to keep him occupied. I tried to treat them as I would my own children. I made a lot of mistakes, but did the best I could under the circumstances. They both became good men, and I hope they have happy, productive lives.

As the years went by, I was becoming more and more immobile. When I got sick, it would turn badly very quickly. After one bout with the flu, I ended up in the hospital with a kidney infection. In the hospital, they wheeled a large digital scale up to my room to weigh me. I couldn't believe it when they told me I weighed 300 pounds more than I had before my injuries. I knew they had to be wrong. It was a number that I just couldn't comprehend. I was mortified, humiliated, embarrassed, and just plain mad.

After that, I didn't even pretend to care about what I ate. I figured that it made no difference. I began to get out less and less. I became an angry and bitter woman. I would have taken my own life, but I didn't care enough about life to bother. Living was a bigger punishment, so why commit suicide and put myself out of my misery when I wanted to be as miserable as possible. All I wanted to do was hide in my home. My life couldn't have gotten any worse.

Chapter 56: Is this the end?

Holidays. I have hated them ever since my father died. When I escaped to Florida, I was relieved of spending holidays with my family. I didn't have to worry about what I looked like or was wearing. I didn't have to worry about who was going to tease me about what. I mostly didn't have to worry about not living up to what everyone had expected of me. I had been in Florida over 5 years when my mother called and said she was moving there. I felt like a black hole was collapsing around me. In Florida, I had been able to spend my holidays at home relaxing, or we would have a picnic lunches at the beach. That ended.

The holidays became horribly stressful instead of relaxing. The stress I felt wasn't from being expected to do something I wasn't capable of. The stress came from the conflict I felt at being expected to do something that I just didn't want to. I had to make command performances every Thanksgiving and Christmas and Mother's Day and birthdays. I was spiraling down after just 2 years of these expectations. Two days before thanksgiving 2001, I started having chest pains.

They started under my breast bone. Then they started radiating up my chest to my throat. There comes that point where you just know that you need to go to the hospital. I had enough sports injuries growing up that I had spent a lot of time in emergency room waiting areas. I think my biggest fears came when I was rushed to the back of the emergency room and didn't have to wait. Then they gave me a nitro pill under my tongue. I'd seen enough hospital shows on television to know what that meant. It didn't work. That's when I really started to get scared. I asked for them to call my priest.

After many hours of testing and adjusting of medication, it turned out that I wasn't having a heart attack. I was having an angina attack. My blood pressure was through the roof. I went to ICU, got stabilized on an ace inhibitor and an angina medicine then was released. In the hospital they couldn't do an echo cardiogram because my fat was too thick for a good signal. No stress test either. I was either too large for the equipment, or they just were afraid the stress test would cause a heart attack. I couldn't even have an angiogram. My leg was too fat to safely insert the catheter.

The cardiologist acted like he didn't want to look at me or touch me. I was now used to that treatment from doctors. He told me that he could put a Band-Aid on the problem, but my "character was so flawed" that he really couldn't help me. He basically wanted me to stabilize quickly so that he could get me off his service. He expected me to go home to die. I can truthfully say that I hadn't been that angry in many years.

One thing they did was take me off the medication that had been controlling or containing my PTSD symptoms to a certain extent. The medication was shown to cause heart problems, not the kind I had, but also was shown to cause large weight gains. The first change I found after going off that medication, and going on the high blood pressure and angina medication, is that I just felt better. I immediately seemed to have more energy, and a brighter outlook. I also just seemed to be able to think clearer. That was a double edged sword.

My personal doctor had to take a closer look at my overall health situation. He ordered up extensive blood work. He ordered the tests that Robin had wanted me to have years before. She was right. There was also something wrong with my thyroid. It took quite a balancing act with my medications because thyroid medication can make your blood pressure go up. After adding the thyroid, the difference was amazing. My hair quit falling out, and I stopped feeling cold all the time. I actually started feeling the heat of living in Florida.

Chapter 57: September 11th

My hospital stay was 6 weeks after the 9/11 attacks. I remember watching the towers fall on television. My father had been raised in Manhattan. Every time NYC was on TV we had to watch. He would point out places he had played at or had jobs at in the background of a parade. We were glued to the tube for the bicentennial celebration. The reopening of the Statue of Liberty was one of the last things we watched before he died. I remember thinking how horrified he would have been. His Grandfather and uncles had been New York City policemen.

My brother and I had taken a trip to visit relatives in New York City in 1990. I remember taking a picture of the World Trade Center looking up. For a kid from the flatlands, it seemed like it must touch the heavens. I was afraid to go up in it. While everyone else in the country was trying to figure out whom to be mad at about it, I was actually mad at myself. I had always been a firm believer that if you aren't part of the solution, you are part of the problem.

I was exactly the kind of person that the rest of the world pointed at to show what is wrong with America. I had allowed myself to vegetate and produced nothing for society. I wanted to be able to help dig through the rubble at ground zero. There was a time I would have volunteered to help, but now, I did good to make it to the bathroom by myself. I knew it was time for me to make my outside look more like what I had always seen my inside to be. It was the beginning of an internal conflict that came to an explosion the day I went to the hospital. I wanted to transform myself into an example of what is right with America. I wanted to be part of the solution. I felt like I had wasted half of my life, and I wanted to save the second half. It didn't matter that my disabilities weren't my fault; I had made bad decisions on how to deal with my disabilities. I wanted to be a contributing member of society again. The problem I had was I didn't know how I was going to do it.

Chapter 58: Out of the Coma

Research was something I had always been good at. Now I was going to have to do research to save my own life. I read every book I could get my hands on about nutrition. It quickly became apparent why the cardiologist in the hospital had been so negative. People my size just didn't lose weight and keep it off without some kind of radical surgery. I had done enough damage to my body without rearranging my plumbing. I was going to treat the whole thing like a science experiment. I was going to try things. If they didn't work, I'd try something else until I finally found something that would work.

I knew I had to have some sort of exercise as a component of this plan to get healthy. I couldn't just hop up and go jogging like I had when I was younger. I would have been too self-conscience at this point to go swimming. This was a road block that had been in my path for a long time. One day I just decided that instead of making a list of what I could no longer do, I decided to make a list of what I might be able to do. I felt like any movement was a good thing. I started by just moving my legs back and forth, like a pair of scissors, while lying in bed. I decided the best way to record what I was doing was with a stop watch. I started by doing it 5 minutes at a time. I also found that I could lay face down across my bed and do flutter kicks like in a swimming pool. I also put a stop watch to that. I just tried to do something everyday, and slowly increased the amount of time I could do each exercise.

One day, I was of course lying in bed, and I was trying to reach my blanket at the end. I repeatedly reached for it and missed. It dawned on me that I was doing a sit up. I tried to do some more. I did 10 then 20. Within a month, I was doing 600 a day. It was amazing, I was finally losing weight.

Eventually, I had a doctor's appointment. I was used to just buzzing by the scales because I was too large for them. The nurse asked me if I had been weighed lately. I told her I had weighed that morning, and what the scale had said. She looked at me and asked sheepishly, "is that good news or bad news?" I told her that meant I had lost a total of 158 pounds. That brought a reaction. The physician's assistant came in to take down everything I was doing. His practice has a lot of really overweight people. The last thing I expected was to be the center of positive attention at the doctor's office.

Whenever I did feel like giving up, something came around to help me. I had a week where I had worked really hard, but didn't lose any weight. I became practically despondent, but then I saw a show on TV that refocused me. I was watching a 3rd anniversary special about the World Trade Center attacks. They were interviewing survivors who had been the last ones out of the buildings. One man had been on a very high floor, and had started to walk down when a largely obese woman passed him going up. She convinced many of his co-workers to try for the roof instead. She was sure that they would be evacuated by helicopter. They didn't know that the doors to the roofs had been bolted because the city had long ago decided that roof top rescues were impractical and dangerous. My reaction to the story was if I had been presented with a 10 flight walk-up or a 90 floor walk down, I would have told myself anything to justify the shorter route.

That woman, and all the people she convinced to go up, died. I thought about myself. I would have died trying to make either escape. I also would have probably taken other people with me. I would have blocked the stairwell. I would have slowed everyone behind me down. It made me start to think about the people whose lives I had touched negatively. I visualized the paramedic loading me in an ambulance suffering a back injury. I imagined someone dying of a heart attack because an ambulance didn't get to him in time because it took two to transport me home. I don't know if either happened, but they could have. In an emergency situation, my size would not only probably get me killed, but might also get another innocent person killed. I couldn't stand the thought. I decided that having one week that I didn't lose weight wouldn't stop me from becoming the person I needed to be.

Chapter 58: Dealing with the Boggart

There were many hurdles that I would have to overcome, but I knew that I would eventually have to deal with some of the issues that caused this mess in the first place. I ate to avoid feeling. I sedated myself with food. I would have to start allowing myself to feel. I had been avoiding my biggest demons. Without the medication and food keeping my PTSD at bay, I started to have floods of flashbacks, memories and nightmares. I became so hyper-vigilant that the smallest of sounds coming from outside our apartment door scared me. I knew I couldn't tackle everything at once, so I started trying to adapt to things in small bites.

When I had gotten so immobile that going to mass became almost impossible, I had started listening to the mass every day on the radio. It obviously wasn't the same, but it was something. It was broadcast on a station owned by the diocese. Most of the air time was devoted to Contemporary Christian music, but the rest of the time was filled with things like the rosary, and devotional prayers. They even had a question and answer time with the bishop. I found myself listening to the music more and more in between listening to the other programming. I seemed to become much calmer when the music was on. I still rely on music.

I had only tried therapy once before in my life, after my father died. I had a really horrible experience. I had chosen a therapist who was a former nun. I thought that meant I could trust her. She turned out to be one of those new-ager types. After several months of increasingly stranger sessions, I decided to investigate her credentials. I found out she had none. In Oklahoma at the time, you weren't required to have a license to do therapy. Her bachelor's degree was in music, and she had taught grade school band in a parochial school. After she left the convent, she received a master's degree in human relations. Her primary practice was with recovering alcoholics, since she was one herself.

So with that bad experience in my past, I knew that if I was to go down that path again, it had better be done right this time. I called a friend who did some volunteer work with Catholic Charities, and asked him about the counselors they had there. He actually recommended a nun who worked out of St. Anthony's. My first thought was, "Great another nun." When I rolled into her office, she sized me up almost immediately saying, "You really don't want to be here do you? So I guess that means you must really need the help."

She had been an OB nurse before her order sent her back to school to get her masters in psychology. She did work with novices, and with the women who were leaving the order. She had originally come to St. Pete to help with the individuals who had been harmed by the clergy abuse scandal. She is cranky and cantankerous, and reminded me of a female Fr. Paul.

We started working together a couple of times a week. She began contacting people who had known me back in Oklahoma. At first I thought she wanted information on if I was who I said I was, but she was actually trying to reconstruct as much as possible about what had happened to me. She wanted to be able to separate which memories and nightmares that I was having were real, and which ones were just nightmares. She and Fr. Paul became regular correspondents. I found it quite irritating to be in her office while she was talking to him on the phone, and laughing about me. I'm pretty sure she knew I found it irritating, and did it on purpose.

She wanted me to go on retreat. I hadn't been on retreat in years. There was a nice monastery just north of St. Pete. They were having a vocations weekend. The monks were very good at what they did. The silence and stillness had a profound effect on me. It brought back all the feelings I once had that I wanted to be a missionary. I signed up to take the lay missionary training. They allowed me to begin the coursework even though they knew I wasn't able to pass the physical part. I would obviously have to learn to walk again.

Sister Anne said that she would recommend me to take a lay overseas assignment if I ever progressed to the point of being able to walk again. I didn't know if I would ever be able to, but it gave me something to dream about. By this time, the boys were both gone. The oldest had entered the US Navy, and the youngest had gone back to live with his father. He was a teenager who needed his dad, and after his older brother left home, he was stuck with two disabled women. With that responsibility no longer on my shoulders, I could focus exclusively on myself for the first time in many years.

Chapter 60: Frankenstein's Monster

When you have a serious disability, it is difficult to know at what point you have accepted your disability in maturity, and when you have just given up hope of getting better. I set my alarm for All Soul's Day so that I could go to morning mass. I always went, no matter what, to pray for my father's soul. When I woke up that morning, something was different. I was different. I was hit with the overwhelming feeling that not only could I get better, that I would get better. It was as if the Lord had healed my spirit, but was leaving the healing of my body up to me.

I had already lost a lot of weight, was doing up to 1400 sit-ups a day. My back muscles and stomach muscles had significantly increased. Somewhere along the way, my back seemed to straighten up. I could almost stand up straight. I decided it was time to try to learn to walk again. I had always been able to walk short distances with difficulty. I could get from my front door to my van. That was maybe 20-30 feet. By the time I got there, I was exhausted and in pain. I used to have to rest for a few minutes before continuing. I realized that I hadn't needed to rest as much lately.

It had been so long since I had been able to do anything except roll around in my wheelchair; I didn't know what I could do. I wanted to stay in motion. Even when tired, I felt like I couldn't sit still. I wanted to walk. It really scared me though. I was afraid that I wouldn't be able to do it. I was afraid I would re-injure my back or my knee and set myself back, maybe permanently. I was afraid that this would be the wall I could not scale. Mostly, I was afraid of the pain.

Instead of stopping at my van when I was headed somewhere, I began to walk across the street to the newspaper box to read the headline. I did that for several weeks. My dog loved it. He seemed excited for me to be doing something different, because that meant he got to smell new smells. My legs hurt. I asked my doctor about the pain. He wanted me to try to walk if I felt like I could without hurting myself. The pain was from the atrophy of the muscles and tendons.

So I tried to walk. At first I walked like a toddler or Frankenstein's monster, nothing would bend. I walked in the alley behind my apartment. It was cobblestone, and I had forgotten how pretty St. Pete was. I marveled at the smells of the orange blossoms and salt air. I lost myself in the green all around me. I lived in the historic old NE neighborhood. It was full of such architectural gems. At first all I could do was walk half way down the block and back. My landlord had a workshop in the carriage house behind the building. After a couple of trips down the alley, I noticed that he was watching me. I never asked if he was watching me in wonder, or waiting for me to fall.

After several months, I was still just walking to the end of my block and back. I would do the same half block several times in a row. I was afraid to go any further away. I was afraid of falling. I was afraid of getting too tired, or in too much pain, and just collapsing. I knew I was pushing myself too hard at times. I would come in and just collapse onto my bed. Some nights I was in so much pain that I couldn't sleep. I just couldn't bring myself to fill a prescription for pain killers. I did begin to allow myself 2 Tylenols a day, mostly so that I could walk farther.

Eventually I knew that I would have to leave my comfort zone. I had been walking my dog the short distance back and forth in my alley without trouble. It was time to see what I could do. I got out the map of our neighborhood and a ruler. I knew that 12 blocks the long way was a mile. There was a bus stop bench 2 blocks away. I decided to try for 2 blocks to start. I went up 2 blocks, sat until my heart rate went down, and then walked home. That was a third of a mile.

When I got home I felt like I could go even further. The next day I walked 2 blocks to my bench, sat down, then walked one more block up and back and sat down again. By the time I had gotten home, I had walked 6 blocks, and that was a half a mile. I was stunned. I began to do that every day for a month. I hadn't sat out to walk that far on purpose since college. I felt great. My knee didn't bother me at all which was surprising. My back didn't hurt any more than it did every other day. The sit-ups seemed to be strengthening and straightening my back. I came inside after my walks and took my blood pressure and pulse. It was normal. I felt like my body was giving me permission to continue.

My clothes were getting looser and looser. I began to be able to walk into places that I used to have to use my wheelchair. I still used my chair at times when I could have walked just to keep from overdoing it and injuring my knee or my back. Even so, I was able to experience a freedom that I hadn't in years. I could go someplace, anyplace, when I wanted to. I had the energy to do anything I wanted to. I began to be able to do the simple things that normal-sized, able-bodied people took for granted, like hopping into the shower whenever I felt like it. What was once an all day ordeal became routine again. My stomach no longer rubbed on my steering wheel. People began to notice the change.

Chapter 61: Clown Clothes

Eventually, I had to confront another hurdle. My clothes were getting comedically too large. I understood that my clothes would get bigger. I didn't expect my pants to get longer. I had put a drawstring of small bungee cord in all my pants, so I just kept cinching them up. I was trying to ignore how long my pants were. At least when I had my shoes on, I didn't actually step on my pants bottoms. I hadn't put my shoes on yet one morning, and got up to go to the bathroom, and actually tripped on my pants and fell. A sprained wrist and large bruise on my shin later, I decided to start sewing some new pants.

I had added to my pants patterns over the years a little at a time. Cutting that pattern down was not going to prove to be as easy. I took a pair of pants and put them on inside out. I pinned the inside leg and front and back crotch. I left the outside leg alone so that I wouldn't have to mess with the pocket. I had to take off over 2 inches of the bottom hem. First I stitched the new seams. When it came time to cut the excess off, my hands were actually shaking. There was no going back now.

When I finished the alterations, the pants fit everywhere but the front crotch. For some reason, that area was still too large. It looked like I had made a pair of maternity pants. At least I wouldn't be tripping over the bottoms anymore. I took the extra material I had cut off these pants to use to see how much I needed to cut down my existing pattern. I needed this pattern to be right, because the next thing I needed to sew was a swimsuit.

I had always been a swimmer. I grew up next to a city park that had a junior pool. I learned to swim before I learned to ride a bike. With my orthopedic problems, water aerobics or lap swimming was going to end up being the best next step. I had the material, and I had a pattern I could start with. All I had to do was conquer my fears of entering the YMCA. I had no more excuses. My insurance company would pay for my membership, but I still was so afraid. As I opened up the box with swimsuit material and patterns, I found an old swim suit. I had it made for me about 10 years previous, and had worn it only a few times before it became too small. It was actually too big now. I ended up having to take up the straps a couple of times, and replaced the elastic on the leg openings, but clearly no longer had any excuses.

Chapter 62: The Locker Room

I hadn't been in a locker room since college. I think I would have rather swam with sharks. I finally decided that I would not die of embarrassment. I would face all the hard bodies inside, and if even one of them looked at me sideways, I was going to hold my head up high, and crush them like a bug if necessary. After all that worrying, the locker room was full of old ladies. I was also not even close to being the fattest person in the room. All my fear had been for nothing.

My YMCA had a class 5 days a week called "Happy Hinges" for the elderly and disabled. The pool area near the "zero depth entry" that I liked to call the boat ramp was congested with walkers and scooters. It was like a Luby's Cafeteria on a Sunday afternoon. They stayed in the shallow end, so I had the deep end to myself. I began to just deep water walk. When a swim lap lane became available, I did one lap, and then went back to my water walking. I stayed in the pool an hour that first time. As I was leaving the pool area, I almost ended up in the men's locker room. I decided that as near sighted as I am, that I'd better get a pair of prescription goggles. They sure made a big difference. I even found a penny on the bottom of the pool once.

After about a month, I decided I was ready to try the deep water aerobics class. I had been scared that I couldn't do it. I did fine, and another of my invisible hurdles was cleared. After a month of doing the deep water class, I began going to the regular water aerobics class just before the deep water class. Some days I sailed through both, other days I felt like I was going to collapse of fatigue on the way to the locker room after class. I was slower than almost all the other students at the beginning, but I refused to quit. I wanted to be the kind of person that had no quit in them. I did have to constantly take up my swim suit, almost once a week for the first six weeks or so.

Once I started getting out and going to the YMCA, I began to "go" as hard as I could for as long as I could. I began pushing myself in a way that I hadn't for a very long time. Not all physically, I wasn't overdoing it to the point of injuring myself, but I was trying to retrain my body and mind to be active. I hadn't held a full time job in 13 years at that point. Just setting a schedule to get up and get to the pool on time was like a new experience. I vaguely remembered getting up every morning for work, fighting the traffic, doing errands on my lunch hour. I was just out of practice. It's like a separate set of muscles that I also had to get back in to shape before I could start having a normal life again.

I had to relearn how to talk to strangers again, and deal with people getting physically closer to me. I was used to people keeping at least 10 feet from me. When someone first sat down on the bench next to me in the locker room, I just about jumped to the ceiling. I wasn't used to people in a store smiling at me. All of these things are like lifting weights in the gym. I came home exhausted from the stimulation. I saw a segment on the Early Show once about two women who had lost over 100 pounds after gastric bypass surgery. They talked about how hard the adjustment was because the weight came off so fast. I think, health aside, this is the main problem with gastric bypass.

Taking the weight off slowly allowed me the time to make small adjustments along the way. If I had lost my entire goal of weight in less than a year, I would have been overwhelmed. Just learning to walk again has been an effort, not just physically. I catch myself watching my feet as I walk to make sure I am "doing it right." Pick up your feet, don't shuffle, don't under pronate, don't favor or limp, these things run through my head with each step. The act of putting my shoes on in the locker room after swimming takes thought. All those years the only place I put my shoes on was with one leg up on my bed so I could reach my foot. I actually have to remind myself that I can lean over now to tie my shoe.

There are 1000 things a day that I have to remind myself to do a new way. I'm embarrassed that I allowed myself to become almost bed ridden and so unproductive, but I can't allow myself the chastisement. That's in the past, and I can't change it. What I can do is climb one inch a day out of the hole I made for myself; relearn everything I have forgotten, except the old bad behaviors that put me in the hole in the first place. I am learning many things that I didn't learn the first time through. So, I get tired easily. It is nice to sleep because I actually need it, and not because I am bored or depressed. And it is very nice to be able to finally recognize the difference.

Chapter 62: Half-way Home

I had spent so much of my life hiding things from myself and others, that the therapy was making me feel so "exposed." On the one hand I had to be careful not to let my success make me think that my troubles were over and slide back into my old behaviors. On the other hand, I had to be careful to not let my fear of failure make me give up. Sr. Anne actually made me sit down to make a list of things I could tell people who noticed my weight loss so that I would stop stressing out from the anticipation. I didn't want to lie, or make a big deal of what was a big deal. I would have preferred that no one noticed or made any kind of fuss.

I decided to keep it simple. If someone asked if I had lost some weight, I'd just say yes. I didn't want to admit how much because I really didn't want people to know how much I used to weigh, and I could see their eyes start to do the math. If someone asked how much I had lost or now weighed, I was going to tell them that ladies never discuss their weight. If someone asked how I had done it, I was going to tell them that I was doing it the simple way; I was eating less and exercising more.

If someone asked me what made me decide to do it, I was going to say that I didn't want to die. I believed that these answers would cover 95% of the questions I was going to face. They were simple, and honest, and hopefully blunt enough to stop any follow-up questions. Any compliments that I received would be met with a simple "thank you." Sr. Anne reviewed my list, and then looked at me over the top of her half reading glasses and said, "You're a real hard case, aren't you. I've never seen anyone so afraid of receiving complements that they practically prepare a questionnaire to deal with it."

I was used to her saying such things to me. She never pulled any punches with me, and that was exactly what I needed. To this day she gives tasks that irritate me, and she knows it. She's 10,000 kilometers away now, but can still be just as irritating by instant message or email. She never lets me quit, she never lets me give up on myself, and she never lets me take the easy way out. It takes an old, cranky, hardhead to deal with one.

I began to actually look forward to doctor's appointments. I thought that if there was anything that I was doing that my doctor or his physician's assistant could use to help someone else in a seemingly hopeless situation, then I was serving a real purpose. I wanted to tell people who understood that pain of being a super morbidly obese person, that there was hope. I wanted to tell the world that this could be conquered. If someone as immobile as I had become can turn their life around, then anyone can.

I had still been very careful about how far I was walking from home, not just out of fear of falling, or of the pain, but also fear of getting lost. My roommate had been taking my dog on long walks in the neighborhood, and training him to return home on command. When I had him with me, I felt I could walk farther because I didn't have to worry about getting lost. I could just tell him to bring me home, and he would turn the right direction, and take a straight path home. It was a great comfort. It allowed me to explore farther from home without fear. My dog, Ozzie, loved it too. Every morning we walked along the beach all the way to the palm arboretum. He pulled me along when I needed a little extra help, and sped up when he knew I needed to stretch it out some.

I had been using my wheelchair less and less. It was actually easier to go into small shops and walk than drag my chair out. Some store's aisles were too narrow for my chair anyway. The more I walked into stores, the better I felt. The one disadvantage was that I had always maintained my upper body strength by trying to push my wheelchair myself. I decided that if I started adding a few push-ups to my sit-ups, that should keep my upper body from losing its tone. My entire world revolved around my diet, exercise, and therapy with Sr. Anne. It became my full-time job. I got tunnel vision. I had to.

One afternoon, I had an appointment with the eye doctor. I had ridden the bus, and my appointment ran late. When I came out, I just missed the bus home. It would be an hour until the next one went by. It was summer in Florida, late afternoon, and very humid. I started to walk out of boredom. I told myself that I would walk between bus benches until the next bus came. What happened instead is that I found myself pushing on. I kept going, block after block. Before long, I looked up and realized I was almost home. It was well over 2 miles from my doctor's office to my apartment. When I finally came in the front door, I fell to my knees, not out of fatigue or pain, but out of gratitude. I had been so blessed. It was at that point that I knew I was going to get a second chance at life.

    The next day, I went down and donated my wheelchair to charity. I no longer needed the security of keeping it. The drop off point was in a converted garage. I saw the attendant roll it inside the door and across to the other side. The floor was sloped to the middle, and as I started to turn to walk away, I saw my chair turn, and begin to roll back towards me. It seemed to be like a child that was being dropped off for the first day of school running back towards their departing parents. It had been my constant companion for 8 long years. The sides of my thighs are permanently indented where the arms rubbed them. So in a way, it will always be with me. I carry the original prescription for the wheelchair in my wallet. I never want to forget.

    It had taken a lot of adjustment to life sitting down, now I was trying to re-learn how to live my life standing up again. The first time I went to buy groceries without my wheelchair, I couldn't find anything. I had been using the same grocery store for several years, but my view had been from 4 feet above ground. I found myself leaning over in the aisle in order to find the things I was looking for. I made it to the check out stand, where once I was confined behind the checkout shelves, I could now see over them. I could once again see over the top of the head of the cashier. I started to feel the room spin and had to shut my eyes. I was actually getting a vertigo episode, a fear of heights almost, from my natural height. That was weird.

    During this time, I was able to reduce the dosage on my blood pressure medicine 6 times. That was a big step towards being able to discontinue it all together hopefully in the future. The more weight I lost, and the more exercise I got, the more energy I had. I wanted to clean all the time. I had 15 years worth of accumulated dirt, clutter, and outgrown stuff that I had just been moving around. I remember how my father had let things like car maintenance go undone in the months before he died. I had literally done that for 15 years. I had spent my time reacting to life instead of acting. Vehicle maintenance went undone, projects were started but never finished, and I had moved my undone failures around with me wherever we went. Going through these boxes of unfinished dreams was painful.

    I had to confront each demon one at a time. For example, I remember the day that I put window tint on my van windows. Always the perfectionist, I have always hated having something not turn out looking like a professional job. The window I did with the end of the roll had creases showing in the film. I decided to leave it like it was. It still did the job that it is designed to do, and the creases were my fault. I had bought the tinting over 5 years before, and had never gotten around to doing the job. Finishing this one job was more important to me than my perfectionism. Each project I finished, each photo I put in an album, every box of unused things sent to the thrift store, was a small victory in my journey to become the woman I was before I became buried underneath all this weight.

Chapter 64: What I want to be when I grow up

I kept working with Sr. Anne on adjusting to my new changed reality. That seemed to take up most of our therapy sessions. I didn't like to call it therapy. I preferred to call it spiritual direction. She didn't mind. She had continued to receive information on my past. One afternoon when I showed up for my appointment, she looked really upset. I thought I had done something wrong to upset her. She had received a call from the attorney representing someone that I may have met at the farm. They had found me because of her inquiries about police reports and case files. He wanted to call me to give a deposition. I had to explain to this attorney that I didn't remember ever meeting his client, and that my brain injury would make any testimony I gave about that time in my life quite inadmissible.

I had been careful about not having my address posted. I received all my mail through a private post office box. All the utilities and leases had been in my roommate's name. I had felt safe for a very long time. All of a sudden, the old fears came flooding back. Sister Anne could tell I was very upset. She arranged for me to go on another long retreat. She wanted me to mingle with people. I had avoided contact out of fear for so long, that it was time for me to learn how to re-engage. The monks recommended a website for Catholics. I had just begun to learn how to use the internet, mostly because that is the primary way that sailors communicate back home.

It allowed me to learn to communicate with new people in a safe environment. It was like instantaneous penpals. I got to debate theology. I made friends with Navy Moms all over the state and country. I was also able to connect with other people facing the prospect of having to lose large amounts of weight. It made my roommate very uncomfortable. One afternoon when I was having lunch with Sr. Anne she mentioned that she had called to tell me something one morning while I was at the gym. My roommate said some really nasty things about me on the phone.

I was shocked. She had a lot of problems, both physical and mental, but we had always co-existed well, and I felt that we had supported each other when we had no one else around to depend on. I was saddened by the realization that some of my isolation may not have been of my own making. I decided I needed to take a long vacation. I hadn't had one in so long, I had no idea where I wanted to go, or even what I wanted to do. I finally decided to take a trip to visit one of my new internet friends. It was the biggest risk I had taken since I had moved to Florida.

Sr. Anne was pretty concerned about the idea at first. She was afraid that I might be putting myself in danger, and apparently she had discovered from talking to my old friends from Oklahoma that I used to have a propensity to take risks. She did a full background check on everyone involved, and only after being completely convinced of my safety, did she give her approval. I thought at one point that she was actually going to go along for the ride as a chaperone. I hadn't been that excited in a long time. Just to be doing something new, going somewhere I had never been before was invigorating.

Chapter 65: Cobwebs

I remember taking long bus trips as a kid. I loved them. I have always loved travel. It was my first trip outside of the country in a very long time. I certainly didn't want to fly. I have never really liked flying, and I was also excited at the idea of seeing parts of the country I hadn't seen in a long time. It was only 5 days on a bus one way. I'd done that as a teenager in old school buses, so a big comfortable Greyhound was going to be a snap. The fact that I had only been walking again for less than a year didn't dissuade me in the least. I had been almost confined to my neighborhood for so many years that the new freedom of being able to go places was intoxicating.

The trip was long, and tiring, but brilliant. I got to see newly released prisoners get on the bus in Georgia, some Amish in Chicago, and some she-males running wild through the bus station in Winnipeg. I also got to see my first snow fall in over a decade in Calgary. I had lived a very sheltered life in many ways for a long time. The trip seemed to stimulate all of my senses. The first night after I arrived was filled with nightmares. These were different. They were vivid. I began to write down what I was remembering. Within the next several months, I would remember almost everything that happened during my attack, except for the face of the man who hurt me.

For so many years, I had not really known what to believe. I had trouble trusting my own memory. Hearing the man's voice for the first time since that night, terrified me. I didn't want to remember. All those years of trying to remember, and now that I could, I didn't want to. When I returned to St. Pete, I read my journal to Sister Anne, a list of images, sounds, feelings, and even smells. She sat in silence for over an hour while I documented the things I had remembered. Finally she opened her eyes, looked over her intertwined fingers, and said, "Almost everything you have remembered matches with what I have been able to reconstruct, except for the attack itself. You were the only witness to that. You are beginning to reclaim what was taken from you, so now what do plan to do with it?"

To my horror, I realized that I didn't know what that was going to mean. What was I going to do with the rest of my life? I had no real idea of what I was actually capable of anymore. She sent me off to a vocational rehabilitation counselor to see how much else I had regained. My memory still had large gaps, especially from my childhood. I could retain new information, but had difficulty maintaining my concentration. I still refuse to use the telephone, which seems to be the strangest thing of all to most people.

I was at that point again of looking not at what I could no longer do, but rather, what I still could do. Of the things I could still do, I had to decide what I really wanted to do. All I knew is that I wanted to sing in church again. I wanted to be a contributing member of society again. After my trip, one thing was also very clear, I was in love. That was the most unexpected thing of all.

Epilogue

I still live a somewhat quiet life. My friends back home were right about one thing. The right man would come along eventually. Luckily, I didn't tell him to take a hike when he did. With his encouragement, I was able to finish my Pastoral Ministry degree. It was just one of a hundred little things that I felt my injuries had robbed me of. Finally being able to finish made me feel like I could reclaim all the parts of my life that had been taken from me.

In all of the discussions I had with Fr. Paul about marriage, one stands out. We were watching the movie "Ryan's Daughter" on St. Patrick's Day one year. In it the Irish parish priest tells a bride to be that the three reasons for marriage are for the production of and rearing of Catholic children, the satisfaction of the flesh, and for companionship on long, cold winter nights. Fr. Paul's comment was "rightly so, rightly so," and he proceeded to give me another one of his long lectures on why I should get married.

Where I live now, the winters are very long, and very cold, and I was reminded of our conversation just this morning. With marriage, almost everyday you can have a revelation about God touching your lives and your marriage. This morning my husband was warming his feet up on mine, and as I felt the warmth from my feet go to his and the temperatures between our feet equalize, I realized that becoming one flesh can mean so many more things than just sexual. Fr. Paul was right about marriage being good for me. He and my Godmother lived long enough to see me safe, married, and on the road to finally healing in both body and soul. Sometimes as I am walking down that road, I catch myself watching my feet in amazement. Friends will offer to give me rides, but I revel in walking, even in winter. Every step I take is a precious gift from God. I hope to never lose sight of that again. After all, my best revenge is a long life, lived to its fullest and filled with God's grace.

When you're first learning to hit the curveball the hardest thing to do is stay in the batter's box. At first the pitch looks like it is going to hit you. If you bail out of the batter's box, it may still curve across the plate for a strike. If you stay put, it might hit you, but even if it does, it won't hurt as bad as a fastball can. You have to overcome your fear of the pain, stay in the box, wait for the pitch to finish, and then hit the stuffing out of it. Learning to be patient and not to fear pain, takes a lifetime to master, and sometimes, you have to take one for the team.

Finis

GLOSSARY

Camp Fire Girls- A youth organization now know as Camp Fire USA that is for boys and girls ages up to 21.

CCD- Confraternity of Christian Doctrine. Common name given to parish based religious education programs.

FmHA- Farmers Home Administration. Governmental organization that provides guaranteed loans in rural areas.

Knight's of Columbus- Organization of Catholic men dedicated to charity, unity, fraternity, patriotism, and family life.

LSAT- Law School Admission Test. Test required for admission to all American Bar Association approved law schools.

Memorare- a popular Marian prayer attributed to St. Bernard of Clairvaux.

Miranda- A warning given by law enforcement officials before questioning criminal suspects in custodial situations.

OSS- Office of Strategic Services. An American intelligence agency formed during World War II. The predecessor to the Central Intelligence Agency.

ROTC- Reserve Officer Training Corps. A college program for the commissioning of military officers.

TPA- Tissue plasminogen activator. A clot dissolving agent approved for use in certain patients having a heart attack or stroke.

VA- United States Department of Veteran's Affairs. Formerly called the Veterans Administration. Governmental organization that administers a variety of veteran's benefit programs including guaranteeing real estate loans.

VFW- Veteran's of Foreign Wars. A US patriotic organization open to honorably discharged US Armed Forces personnel who served in a foreign zone during an armed conflict. The Women's Auxiliary component is open to the wives, daughters, mothers and sisters of VFW eligible personnel, living or dead.

The Author:

Catherine Mardon was born and raised in Oklahoma City, Oklahoma. She holds a BSci in Agriculture (Forestry) from Oklahoma State University, a BA in Pastoral Ministry from Newman University (Kansas), a JD from the University Of Oklahoma College Of Law, and is currently pursuing a Masters of Theological Studies degree. She is happily married and is an active member of her parish and community. She continues to work daily on her recovery from the debilitating injuries she received, and still fights for social justice issues.